be kept

# THE NEW AMERICAN QUILT

## An Innovation in Contemporary
## Quilt Design

# THE NEW AMERICAN QUILT

## An Innovation in Contemporary Quilt Design

## by Margit Echols

Doubleday & Company, Inc.
Garden City, New York
1976

Library of Congress Cataloging in Publication Data

Echols, Margit.
    The new American quilt.

    1. Quilting—Patterns.    I. Title.
TT835.E36      746.9′7
ISBN 0-385-09924-X
Library of Congress Catalog Card Number 76–2839

Copyright © 1976 by Margit Echols
All Rights Reserved
Printed in the United States of America
First Edition

*To my teachers*
*Esther Small*
*Jean Wnuk*
*and Mary Ann*

Photography by Stuart Chasmar
Embroidery by Libbie Flanagan
Black/white and color processing by MODERNAGE

Special thanks to my editor Jean Bennett, to the Lower East Harlem Community Quilters for my background in quiltmaking, and to Arnold Galvez and the Volunteer Urban Consulting Group for their unfailing assistance to the Lower East Harlem Community Quilters. Also to Christian Schieldrop for talking me down.

Patterns, drawings, and creation of City Quilts I and II by the author

# Contents

# THE NEW AMERICAN QUILT

## An Innovation in Contemporary Quilt Design

# CHAPTER 1

# An Introduction to Design

Most modern quilters have relied on design ideas and patterns from the past, but originally quilters created their designs from their own experience and environment. The intention of this book is to go back to that principle of quilt-making and show how you can create your own quilt designs using objects, places, or events that have some significance for you. The world around you can provide unlimited ideas. Equally unlimited are the possibilities for abstract designs, using different shapes and colors in innumerable combinations.

The design of a quilt can have many origins. Sometimes it's as simple as starting with fabrics you especially like and putting them together in the combinations, shapes, and sizes that are most pleasing. Other times you'll start with an empty space and invent a design, then choose the colors and fabrics which seem best for it.

Trying a variation on a traditional pattern is always a good way to learn, by experience, basic design principles. Occasionally, I'll use traditional patterns for individual blocks or squares and assemble the finished ones in a new way, or I may add to or change the original squares and then assemble them. Once I spent hours juggling the colors and prints I had until I found a way of putting them together that worked well. Later I found that, with one addition, I'd "created" a very old design called "puss in the corner." This shows how innate basic principles of design really are; I can create a design similar to one originated by someone else long ago because those basic principles—what works and what doesn't and what works best of all—are timeless.

If you're starting with an empty space, the first step is to decide the size and shape of the full quilt. You'll develop your design within that space. If the quilt is going to be made up of individual blocks of the same or varying patterns, make each block exactly to size, so that it can be used to make the working pattern. Chapter 3 will show you how to make the pattern from your master drawing. If the quilt consists of just one large subject, you can draw it to scale and then enlarge it by using a grid or an opaque projector.

After you've decided the size and proportions of the space you're working with, you can begin to experiment with design. If you're interested in doing something geometric, try looking through a few books on geometry until something triggers your imagination, and then make up your own design. Or start cutting up the space with a pencil or a pair of scissors. Or buy a box of Coloraid paper, cut out some shapes from your favorite colors, and experiment by moving them around within the space. Or look through a kaleidoscope, or think of children's blocks. Try folding à la origami, or fold some plain paper and cut out snowflakes. Use one as the design for a whole quilt, or use twelve or sixteen or twenty, all different, for an appliquéd quilt. There are really no limits to the possibilities in design.

The point is, the more you experiment with design the more you'll see and understand how it works; once you begin to discover your own special relationship to it, there'll be no limit to the creative possibilities. You can go ahead and make your own quilt revolution.

The Bradshaw Quilt was done for my friend Michael Bradshaw, who had chosen the colors and design he liked best; together we worked for hours to come up with the arrangement that is uniquely his. When the quilt was finished and on his bed it looked as though it belonged there and nowhere else. I'll never make another just like that (color plate 5). Belinda Gray, at Lower East Harlem Community Quilters, used the same design for her choice of solid colors which has, of course, been named Belinda (color plate 6). It's interesting how different it looks compared to the Bradshaw Quilt, and it's a beauty. There are as many possible variations on that pattern as there are people who will use it.

An important point to remember in creating your own design is that you are not bound to follow your original idea if it's not working the way you thought it would; feel free to change it as you go along.

In the process of designing you will also be concerned with the purpose of the quilt. Maybe you want to make a quilt to celebrate a marriage, cover your new baby, please a bachelor . . . the possibilities go on and on. When dealing with personalities and tastes besides your own you'll work around the person who will be its owner. For yourself, maybe you'll fulfill a fantasy you've al-

2

ways had about what your bedroom should look like, and make a quilt of silk and satin, ribbons and lace. Maybe you'll want to make a quilt that spells someone's name in big block letters. Whatever your idea, don't let your design be restricted by lack of technical know-how; that's what this book is about, and expertise will come with doing.

# CHAPTER 2

# The City Quilt and the Country Quilt

Most American quilts, particularly the old ones, come from the country. Quilting was probably for the most part an occupation for the winter, which brought its own kind of confinement. Summer was hot and hands were needed for other things. The designs usually reflected the lives of the women who made them. When they weren't abstract, they were of flowers, birds, animals, schools, and farmhouses or other country themes. Their lives, families, and religion as well as their clothes went into those quilts, which have finally come to be considered works of art. Quilts like these are still being made, the patterns passed from generation to generation. They are still beautiful and still part of that world, which is probably why quiltmaking is associated so strongly with the country. People who are city born and bred don't feel an emotional link with the process of making a quilt, although they may enjoy owning one. The rhythm of their daily lives is different, as well as their needs and pastimes.

City life has different roots and different pressures. Women don't sew as much as they used to and when they do, they're not in the habit of saving the scraps out of severe economic necessity. How many urban women are patient enough or have the time to spend the hours it takes to sew a quilt together, especially by hand? Nevertheless, there is an increasing need to regain a bit of the past and feel a part of this country's tradition. People want to use their hands again, and the more quiltmaking becomes a part of city life, the more comfortable city women will feel about it being a part of them, too.

There is no need to feel diffident about making use of design ideas that reflect our lives and our technology. Many of us are not surrounded by trees, flowers, and fields. We live in the midst of traffic and tall buildings, crowded with everyday things that are peculiar to us and our time. The patterns in this book are for my own City Quilt, which serves as an example of the translation of an environment and life-style into a contemporary, personal quilt design (color plates 2 and 3). Unfortunately, the things one sees every day slip into the subconscious and stay there, taken very much for granted. When I began the pattern for the traffic light, for instance, I realized I had no idea what it really looked like. I tried to sketch a brownstone from memory and couldn't. Then I started walking around the city, studying the shapes and colors of very simple things, and I discovered how beautiful they can be. Traffic signs are designed to be clear and readable, and their simplicity is striking. Many other man-made objects that are meant to be purely functional are superior in design and will make good subjects for quilt designs.

Traditional quilts are lovely, and more often than not they're my favorites. But my pleasure in making quilts is not in repeating designs that have been done and done before. It is in experimenting with my own. Some people prefer to use patterns that have already been worked out, which is easily understandable, since designing brings with it its own set of problems. Their pleasure is in the tiny stitches they take by hand as they pass the time of day with their families or friends. They can get plenty of variety in their quilts by trading patterns with other quilters and by changing the color combinations and materials they use. But if you do have the urge to experiment, don't feel limited by traditional designs and styles. Quilts are a form of creative expression, and any design that comes from you and is pleasing to you is right. The only basic requirement is consistency in the quality of workmanship. If the work is sloppy, the quilt will show it no matter how beautiful or innovative the design may be. Many quilts are prized for their workmanship alone. If your work is neat, go ahead and experiment as much as you like with design.

The thirty designs taken from city life included in this book illustrate how much can be done with a single theme or idea—anything can be the source of inspiration for a beautiful or unusual quilt design. If you want to do a quilt with city patterns, those in this book are drawn so they can be traced and taken directly from the book. If you want to design your own patterns, Chapter 3 will show you a quick technique for patternmaking that will enable you to start making your own patterns right away.

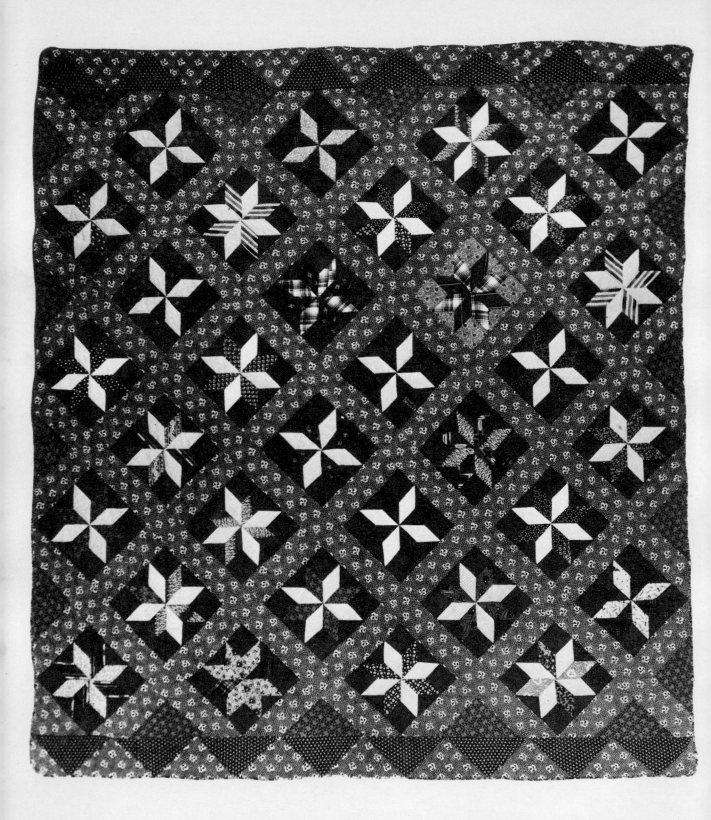

*Antique quilt from the collection of the author. The strips used to separate the blocks form a diamond pattern.*

Alice's Star, *quilt designed by Alice Phillips of Lower East Harlem Community Quilters, demonstrates the use of separators in a square block pattern.*

# COMMUNITY QUILTS

Quilting is a great way for an urban group to celebrate itself or an event. With the patterns in this book I've intended to provide a departure from traditional quilt design that reflects another aspect of life in this country. A community group should design squares about itself. If it's a very poor one and the purpose of the quilt is in some way political, the designs can describe aspects of its condition, or hopes of its improvement. The Hudson River Quilt is a superior work of art and a good example of how a quilt can make a statement or express an opinion. This can be done through the choice of colors, somber or gay, or by depicting local incidents, landmarks, or current events. The quilt may also reflect the pride a community takes in itself and its condition, rich or poor. More and more community quilting groups, urban as well as rural, are sitting down together to sew quilts which are expressions of their unique environment.

Quilting can be a social event for senior citizens, YWCAs, Girl Scouts, Lions Clubs, prisons, schools, or any other type of gathering. Making a quilt is also a good way to learn to sew and see immediate results. People respond to pictures, and a great deal of the tedium so often associated with quiltmaking has been eliminated by modern sewing practices.

## THE NEW YORK CITY BICENTENNIAL QUILT

The making of the New York City Bicentennial Quilt was the result of a course sponsored by the New York City Bicentennial Corporation, the School Art League, and the Lower East Harlem Community Quilters. It was meant to commemorate New York's celebration of the Bicentennial. This first course was intended to nudge the Board of Education into including quiltmaking as an American art and tradition in the standard junior high and high school curricula, and to encourage senior citizens and their groups to

*The Hudson River Quilt, started in 1969, has thirty squares, each designed by a different woman. The group was drawn together by Irene Preston Miller, who was involved in both conservation and textiles and had the idea of a quilt as a means of making a statement on the conservation of the Hudson River. Only a few of this group had any quilting experience, but careful research on their chosen spot and a desire to do their best on their appliqué and embroidered squares resulted in a unique and striking quilt. The Husdon River Quilt Fund has been created and is supported by the sale of postcards of the quilt and by lending the quilt for exhibition. This fund will contribute in some small way toward the future preservation of the river.*

*New York City Bicentennial Quilt designed by the author. Photo by Richard Gray.*

consider quiltmaking as a possible cottage industry as well as a means of celebrating the Bicentennial.

I decided that the New York City Bicentennial Quilt should document contemporary city life. I wanted to stay away from landmarks as much as possible and focus on the things we come into contact with every day: hot dog stands, taxicabs, garbage cans, street sweepers, tenements. I understood that my students would have varying amounts of experience in sewing. I wanted to create a situation that would make the art of quilting available to them all and provide a basic system of patternmaking and quilt construction that would be fast and accurate enough to give them immediate results. We were also working on a tight schedule, with only fifteen three-hour sessions in which to accomplish the making of the quilt.

The discouraging thing about making a new design is the time it takes to get it from the idea stage into fabric, together with the mystery of exactly *how* to do it. It was important to assure them that these agonies would be minimized. In the end everyone learned how to make a pattern, and for those whose pleasure was simply sewing I provided patterns each week for buildings, buses, signs, cars, and other city subjects they could execute and personalize with embroidered names of their own streets, neighborhoods, and schools.

This book passes on to you the techniques for designing and making quilts which I devised for my classes.

What I enjoyed most was the warm, friendly atmosphere that grew more relaxed and familiar each week. It was nice being around the older women, who gave out a feeling of warmth and approval and gently passed on what they knew to the young whenever their help was needed. The teachers picked up everything quickly and paired off with whoever needed extra help. The young were generally full of energy and had no trouble with the patterns or sewing, even when they'd had no experience, as long as there was someone there to go to with their questions. They adapted easily to the machines and were all impatient to finish their patches so they could see their picture of the city. The older women took over the handwork because it was more their style. They enjoyed taking their time, telling stories while they worked. It was a very pleasant experience and I think the quilt truly benefited from the mixture of ages and preferences. Toward its completion I asked all participants to embroider their names and ages, ranging from eight to eighty-one, on it.

## SCHOOLS

This book is ideal for the classroom because it is a workbook and meant to be nothing else. The instructions have been written to be as clear and concise

*11*

*Katherine Kelly of Lower East Harlem Community Quilters working on the New York City Bicentennial Quilt.*

as possible. Under the guidance of a teacher who has a knowledge of sewing or, better, quiltmaking, there shouldn't be any difficulty in putting together a full-sized quilt. The patterns have been arranged in a specific order beginning with the easiest and progressing to the more complex. If you are a teacher with students of varying experience, let them pick the ones they'd like to tackle most. The student with no experience shouldn't be left out. There are patterns that require little more than taking a ½-inch seam. At first, taking that ½-inch seam may feel very awkward, but given a little practice in using the machine, it won't be long before he will be able to assemble one of the simpler designs. This kind of quiltmaking is certainly easier to learn and gives faster visual results than dressmaking and, as we all know, children are impatient and want to see results right away. Quiltmaking is a good introduction to sewing, and there are many patterns to choose from here that will appeal to a child's imagination. The ambitious student or the one with more experience will want to try one of the more complicated designs. In my first class I had students who knew nothing of quilting and some who did, and some who knew how to sew, and one who could do beautiful embroidery who later in the class took over teaching others how to embroider. In the end, no one was left out. Everyone did at least one square in the finished quilt.

Sometimes two will want to pair up. Let them. It can be very good if they do. If one cuts and hands the pieces to the one at the machine and presses them when they are sewn, the one at the machine won't have to get up all the time to press. Some may prefer cutting and pressing to sewing anyway, and if they work in twos they can help each other with the instructions and enjoy each other's company.

It is advisable to have more than one sewing machine available or only a few will have a chance to sew.

Do not expect anyone to be able to use paper scissors—they are impossible to use on fabric. The scissors must be good and very sharp, or the student won't be able to understand why he's having such a hard time cutting. He'll think there's something wrong with him. Sharp scissors are no more dangerous than a pencil.

Children are very quick and have no trouble following directions as long as there is a teacher around who can answer questions when they have doubts. They will get a great kick out of the "city" designs because they are part of their experience. To make the patterns even more personal they can embroider their names on them, or their street numbers on the houses, familiar destinations on the buses, local titles on the schools, churches or government buildings, and shops. Or, if they are really adventurous, they can draft patterns of their own from scratch using the patternmaking instructions in Chapter 3. The finished quilt can be hung in the school auditorium for display. A quilt about them and their school and their neighborhood is something they will be very proud of.

# ENLARGING A DESIGN

An opaque projector is the easiest way to enlarge a design if you ever have to. The master drawing can be projected on the wall in just about any size you want. Hang up a piece of paper the size of your quilt to be (or newspaper taped together or whatever you have that will serve) and trace out the lines of your drawing from the image the projector has given you. Cut out the pieces after numbering them, indicating which side is the "right" side. When the pattern pieces are this large I leave out the Steps 3 and 4 of the pattern-making formula because they're just too big to handle when it comes to tracing them and adding the ½-inch seam allowance. I simply lay out the pieces on the fabric and add the ½ inch as I cut. When you do this just remember not to leave out the seam allowance.

A grid is more time-consuming, but it works when you don't have a projector. You still need a piece of paper the size you want your finished quilt to be or a makeshift piece made of newspaper or brown wrapping paper taped together. Divide your drawing into ten equal squares and your quilt-size paper into ten equal squares. Copy the drawing onto the big paper, using the grid as a guide. When it looks right to you, number the pieces and mark the "right" side and cut them out. Just as described above, lay them on the fabric you've chosen for each piece and add the ½-inch seam allowance as you cut.

# CHAPTER 3

# Patternmaking for Quilts of Any Design

You don't have to be a great artist to make a drawing for your pattern. You don't even have to sketch well. Think of it as a skeleton on which you're going to build a beautiful quilt block. It is only a practical breakdown of your idea into working pieces.

There are a few things to keep in mind while drafting a pattern. If you want a pattern for patchwork, remember that curves are very hard to sew neatly. They are more easily appliquéd. In appliqué, the edges can be turned under by hand, or the pieces can be faced by machine, then turned and stitched down by hand, whichever you prefer. There are examples in the patterns of the Factory, School Bus, Traffic Light, Armory, Government Building, Shop, Mailbox, 1976, and Hot Dog Wagon. Notice that the other parts of those patterns and the rest of the designs in the book are done in patchwork. The only curved piece that was done in patchwork was the Fire Hydrant, and that was a fairly large one. You'll find, too, that many curves can be squared off in a design and still suggest what they are meant to. Turning corners can also be difficult, so it's wise not to make very sharp angles. The Church, Movie House, Brownstone, and Street Sweeper are examples.

When preparing your sketch, remember that each line will be a sewing line and ask yourself, as you draw, if each seam can be sewn up comfortably. If it can't, you should be able to adjust your pattern without radically altering your original idea. Remember that the background is as much a part of the pattern as the subject. Each piece that is created by the line drawing becomes a piece of fabric later on. Think of it as a puzzle into which all the pieces must fit; without one, the puzzle will be incomplete. The only difference between a puzzle and a pattern is that your pieces will need seam allowances. Seam allowance is explained in Step 4.

*Tools for patternmaking: felt-tip pen, clear plastic ruler, tracing paper, graph paper.*

## THE PATTERNMAKING FORMULA

### STEP 1 *Make a Sketch*

The easiest way to draw it and square it off at the same time is on graph paper with a ⅛-inch rule. Make the pattern any size you want, but remember the smaller it gets, the more difficult the sewing will be later on. If you want

*Margit Echols, Marie Mendico, and Lorraine
Townsend working on the New York City
Bicentennial Quilt. Photo by Jack Lipkins.*

it to match the size of the patterns in this book, draw it within a 10- by 12-inch rectangle. When it is sewn up in the finished quilt, it will measure 9 by 11 inches because a ½-inch seam allowance is "taken up" all the way around.

The graph paper makes the work go quickly and helps save time later on when you add the ½-inch seam allowance.

STEP 2 *Revise for Sewing Ease*

After you're happy with the design, study it and decide which lines will be best extended as seams, if necessary. For example: The line on the bottom of piece 1 of the Stop Sign had to be extended out to the sides to make sewing easier. Otherwise I'd have had to sew around those two bottom corners. It was easier to make two extra pieces.

*Extending the bottom edge of the stop sign on the pattern to create a seam all the way across eliminates the necessity of turning corners on small pieces.*

STEP 3 *Number Each Piece*

Look at your pattern drawing and consider the order in which you will sew up the pieces. There may be several ways. Try to pick the easiest. The more practice you have at doing this, the easier it will become. Number them so they won't get mixed up, and you can refer to the pattern drawing as a guide

*The Hudson River Quilt*

*The City Quilt—Solid Color Version*

*The City Quilt—Print Version*

*The New York City Bicentennial Quilt*

whenever you need to. If the same piece appears twice in the pattern, give it the same number and write on it that it requires two pieces. Then when you cut you will know how many you need.

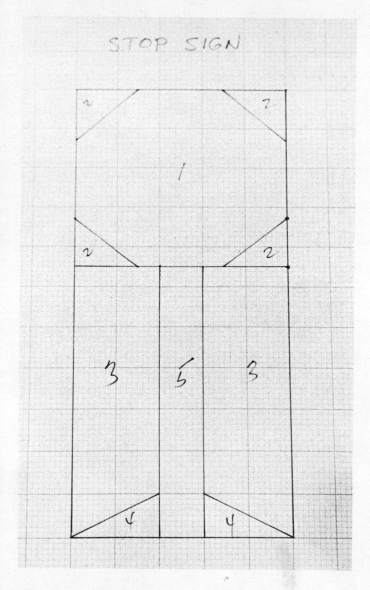

*Numbering the pieces in the order in which they are to be sewn will make assembly easier and faster.*

### STEP 4 *Add Seam Allowance*

Place a piece of tracing paper on top of the drawing. With a ruler, trace accurately around piece 1. Remove the tracing paper and place it over another piece of graph paper, adjusting the lines so the sides of piece 1 are squared with the lines on the graph paper. Anchor in place with a couple of pieces of

*19*

tape. Draw a line precisely ½ inch all the way around piece 1. Use the lines in the graph paper to guide you and a clear plastic ruler to give you the ½-inch lines on angles or any lines that aren't squared with the graph. To use this ruler, simply place it with its center line on top of the line to which you want to add the ½ inch, and trace around the outside edge. Check yourself

*Each pattern piece must be traced separately.*

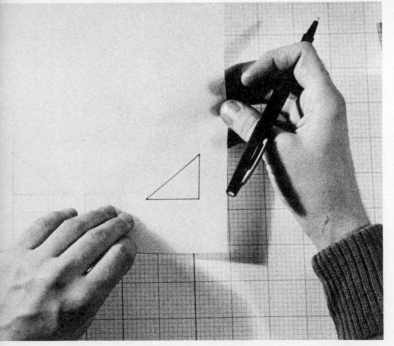

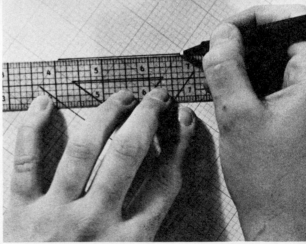

*The tracing is lifted off and repositioned on the graph paper in order to draw the ½-inch seam allowance on each side.*

to see that you've added exactly ½ inch, or you will be off later on when assembling the pieces.

Repeat for each piece. Don't forget any pieces and be sure to number them as you go.

You now have all your pattern pieces and a sewing guide. Choose your colors and cut.

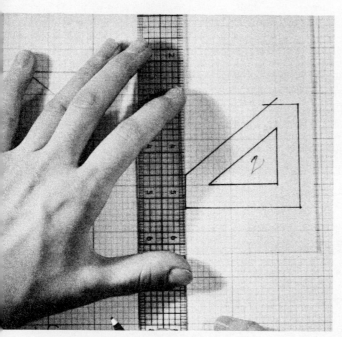

The corners of angles should be squared off after the seam allowance has been drawn.

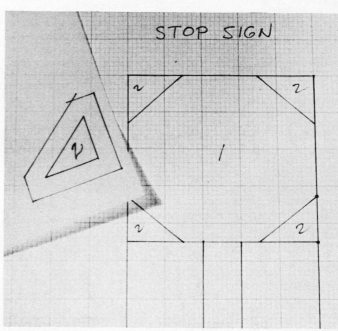

Each pattern piece is numbered to match the master drawing.

## COPYING THE CITY PATTERNS

The easiest way to copy the patterns for immediate use is to Xerox each page. It takes a few seconds and they're ready for use. Just be sure you don't use a machine that makes a reduction in size. If a Xerox machine isn't available, copy them by hand with tracing paper. Copy accurately or the pieces won't fit when you sew them together. If you're in the habit of using ½-inch seams, it's not necessary to trace the "sewing line," which is the thin line ½ inch in from the outside "cutting line." If you'll feel more comfortable with the guideline, it can be transferred to the fabric with a tracing wheel. It is essential, however, that you mark all the notches and fold lines.

To avoid confusion, especially if you're doing more than one pattern at a time, write the name of the design on each pattern piece. If you plan to reuse the patterns, it's a good idea to mount them on stiff paper or cardboard with spray adhesive, rubber cement, or double-faced tape, making sure that each one is properly titled and numbered.

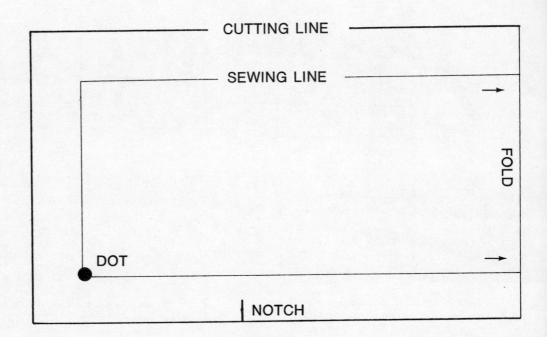

# CHAPTER 4

# Quilt Construction

Patchwork or pieced quilts are generally constructed with straight-edged pieces such as squares and triangles. The seams are hidden, that is, they are on the inside of the quilt. Unlike appliqué, patchwork can be done by machine as well as by hand.

Appliqué is the term used to describe the method of sewing one layer of fabric on top of another. It is done by hand with tiny hem stitches after turning under the edges of the top layer. It is thought that the finer quilts are done this way for weddings and special occasions, and for guests when they come to stay. Machine appliqué does not have the same quality.

Embroidery can be used on quilts as additional decoration to accent the design. It, too, should be done by hand to look its best.

Quilting through is the final process of assembly which fixes the quilt top to its lining, batting, and back. The stitches are put through all layers by hand in a number of patterns and designs. The stitches look best when they are small, neat, and regular. Machine stitching rarely looks as nice as hand stitching for quilting through.

## THE SEWING MACHINE?

For a long time now, there's been an argument about whether or not a quilt is a "real" quilt if any part of it was done by machine. If you enjoy doing everything by hand, including patchwork, for pleasure or because you don't have a machine, that's fine. I appreciate enormously a hand-stitched patchwork quilt, but I would never have the patience to make one, and this is true of a lot of other people today. As far as I'm concerned there is no reason to be ashamed of doing the patchwork seams by machine. Appliqué, embroidery, and quilting through should be done by hand because the result is so much nicer, but patchwork is better done by machine because the seams which are going to take all the stress will be stronger, and visually the effect is the same. If you're planning to sell your quilts, the time saved by machine stitching is crucial.

## NOTCHES

Notches have been drawn on some pattern pieces to make assembly easier. By simply matching notches where indicated, the fitting together of irregularly shaped pieces or curved pieces can be accomplished quickly and without error.

## SEAMS

Although it's more common for quilters to use ¼-inch seams, it's better to use ½-inch seams because they are so much stronger. A ¼-inch seam may pull out, especially in fabric that frays, such as silks, velvets, wools, and some satins. However, a ¼-inch seam is sometimes used for curved or circular pieces which are to be appliquéd, because no strain will be put on them and they'll be less cumbersome to handle.

Unless a ¼-inch seam is specified, always use a ½-inch seam with the city patterns in this book.

## THE FOLD OF THE FABRIC

You will see that some of the patterns are drawn and marked with the word "fold." When a pattern piece is very large it's easier to draw only half of it and place the center line on the fold, making it easier to handle and less cumbersome to cut.

## COLORS, FABRICS, AND YARDAGES

I've done two city quilts from the patterns in this book, one in solid colors and one in prints (color plates 5 and 6). As before, in the Belinda and

Bradshaw quilts, I was delighted to find that each quilt has a personality all its own.

The solid-color quilt reminds me of a child's blocks and poster prints. The print quilt looks old-fashioned even though the designs are modern. Prints and solids together are lovely, and give a third very different effect.

Since a lot of these pattern pieces are small, I would suggest avoiding heavy or bulky fabrics. If this is your first experience making a quilt or you're doing it as a class project, stay absolutely away from flimsy or slippery fabrics such as silk, satin, and velvet. Knits in general are unsuitable, and the thick double knits look awful in quilts. Pure cottons and blends of 50 per cent cotton and 50 per cent dacron or polyester are best for a city quilt, but if you are experienced in working with silk and satin and prefer them to cotton, go ahead.

I would suggest having available a half yard each of a few bright colors such as blue, turquoise, orange, green, dark green, navy blue, brown, yellow, white, black, red, a stripe, and any others that appeal to you. I found I needed two yards of the background color (white) for the big blocks, and two yards for the separators (turquoise). Buy five or six yards for the back and borders, depending on how large the finished quilt is. I used four yards of 48-inch width material for a 64- by 78-inch quilt.

I use a commercial polyester batting for the filler. Several types produced especially for quilts are sold in department and retail stores.


## CUTTING

Cutting must be accurate or the pieces won't fit and there will be lumps and gathers that won't press out. The patterns have been arranged on the pages to make the cutting as easy as possible. I've left no space between the pieces that are to be cut from the same color. This eliminates waste and the time it would take to cut around the edges of each piece separately. All you have to do after copying the page is place it directly on the fabric, usually of double thickness, pin in place through the middle of each piece, and cut along the cutting line. The patterns should be placed as often as possible on the straight grain of the fabric unless cutting on the bias is indicated. The pieces will sew up easier because they won't pull or stretch.

Sometimes one pattern piece will call for two or three pieces cut from the same color or perhaps another cut from a different color. Always be sure to follow the instructions written on each pattern piece carefully. The layout of the pages has been designed with ease of cutting in mind.

After cutting each piece, check and be sure you've clipped the notches, because you'll need them later as sewing guides.

## CONTINUOUS SEWING

If you have a lot of squares or triangles to sew together and you're using a sewing machine, just run them through one after the other without stopping to lift up the foot, take out each piece, trim the thread, and start the next. Sew off the end of each one about an inch, and, without lifting up the foot, slide the next one under and keep going until all your pieces are completed. The thread, you'll notice, twists between each block, and this serves as a knot. When the blocks are done clip the threads and press the pieces. This is an extremely useful technique for the professional quilter who needs to make maximum use of the time available, but leisure-time quilters will also find it handy.

## PRESSING

Pressing seams in one direction is faster, easier, and stronger than pressing each one open. As a general rule, it's a good practice to press a seam in the direction of the darker fabric, especially when the fabric is a little sheer, so that the seam doesn't show through the lighter fabric.

In the instructions for each pattern there will be several pressing steps. If your work is neat it won't be necessary to press except when the instructions indicate. *Never* press silk, satin, or velvet on the right side.

## ASSEMBLING THE BLOCKS

After cutting, leave the pattern pieces pinned to the fabric until you're ready to sew them together. Keep the numbered diagram in front of you for easy reference so you won't have any trouble figuring out which piece goes where. The pieces are numbered, as often as possible, in the order in which they are to be sewn together. This way, assembly should be quick and easy. Have the scissors and the pin box within reach, and keep the iron hot so that it will be ready to use when you need it. Once the pieces are cut it should take only a few minutes to assemble each block. I would suggest assembling the blocks one at a time to avoid getting the pattern pieces mixed up, since each pattern is numbered separately.

When the blocks are sewn up into the finished quilt they will measure 9 by

*Alice Mucha helps find a place for Federal Hall in the New York City Bicentennial Quilt.*

11 inches. The separators (the traffic patterns) will be 5 inches wide. The separators are made with a different background color to set off the larger blocks. For a "city" quilt, this works out very nicely because the 5-inch separators become city streets and the 9- by 11-inch squares city blocks. If you make one each of the 9- by 11-inch patterns and use the 5-inch separators all

27

around the outside of the quilt as well as between the blocks, and arrange the blocks in a grid formation, four across and five down, the finished quilt will measure 61 by 85 inches. If you add a 4-inch border of a contrasting color as I have, the finished size will be 69 by 93 inches. If you want to change the dimensions, use less or more patterns. To make it larger you can make some of the designs twice, in different colors. Or, draft your own additional patterns. By adding blocks you can make the quilt as large as you like. You might use five across and five down, which begins to square it off and requires twenty-five blocks.

You may even decide you don't want a grid design, but a more irregular arrangement, as in the print version of my City Quilt. In any case, you can put the blocks and separators together any way you like. Just remember that the more irregular the design becomes the more difficult it will be to sew up. The New York City Bicentennial Quilt was extremely difficult to assemble since each piece was a different size. It took hours of trial and error before it was right. The result is beautiful, but putting together a quilt that can be sewn up in rows is a lot easier and just as beautiful.


## FINAL ASSEMBLY

After the entire top has been assembled and pressed, you will be ready to put it together with the lining, batting, and the back for the final "quilting through."

A lining under the quilt top absorbs a lot of stress and wear and tear that the top would otherwise have to take. A soft old sheet would be very good for this purpose.

Choose a backing of a bright color that contrasts nicely with the quilt top and looks suitable as a border.

Assuming that the size of the quilt calls for five yards of 48-inch material for lining and backing (excluding lining if you're using an old sheet), cut the five-yard lengths in half and sew them together lengthwise so they measure 90 by 96 inches.

You are now ready to assemble the quilt. This can be done several ways. Some may prefer to place the top, lining, batting, and back on top of each other, pin or baste in place, and roll the quilt in their laps or on a frame. I prefer to use what I call the "pillowcase" method:

Spread the batting out on the floor. Place the lining neatly and squarely on top. Pin around the sides. Place the quilt top on top of that and pin the three layers together. Take the whole piece to the machine and with a ¼-inch seam stitch all around the sides, fixing the layers together.

Spread the quilt out flat on the floor. Place the backing, right side in, on top and pin evenly in place all the way around. Take the whole quilt back to the machine and with a ½-inch seam sew all the way around except for about one yard left open to pull the quilt through to the right side. Before turning it right side out, clip the corners.

After pulling it through close the opening by hand. Put the quilt down again, smooth it out, and pin in place at frequent intervals for the final "quilting through." Then baste. Then have a quilting bee and with small, regular stitches quilt all the layers together, through and through. Quilt across in a grid pattern or around the shapes of the designs.

## THE CARE OF YOUR QUILT

I've learned that cleaning a quilt is a lot safer than washing it. If you do clean it, air it out for a day or so when it comes back to get rid of the smell of the cleaning fluid. If your quilt has a lot of white in it, ask that fresh cleaning fluid be used or it may look a little dingy even though it's clean.

Always clean a silk or velvet quilt. Never wash an old one, silk or cotton, or it will be torn apart. If you do want to have a washable quilt, test each fabric before sewing for shrinkage and color fastness.

CHAPTER 5

# The City Patterns

Detour                  Mailbox
One Way Sign            1976
Stop Sign               Hot Dog Wagon
Arrow                   Shop
Car                     Government Building
                        School Bus
                        Armory or Castle
                        Factory

Subway Car
Subway Tracks
                        Church
                        Street Sweeper
                        Brownstone
Car (side)              Movie House
Mail Truck
Ambulance
Trailer Truck           Fire Hydrant


                        Tenement
Intersection            School
Traffic Light           Hotel
Bus                     Cafe

## DETOUR SIGN

| 1 | 2 | 3 | 2 | 3 | 2 | 3 | 2 | 1 |
| 1 | 2 | 3 | 2 | 3 | 2 | 3 | 2 | 1 |

# DETOUR

Suggested Colors: Black, Yellow
 (Solids or Prints)

**Black:**

Cut four of Pattern 1
Cut six of Pattern 3

**Yellow:**

Cut eight of Pattern 2

## STEP 1

Sew 1 to 2, matching notches.
Sew 3 to 2, matching notches.
Alternate 2 with 3, matching notches, until you have a row of four 2s and three 3s.
Sew a 1 on the other end, matching notches.
This makes one half of the arrow; make the other half the same way, and press both rows.

## STEP 2

Checking diagram, match the two sides of the design and sew together, making a center seam.
Press on both sides.

# DETOUR SIGN

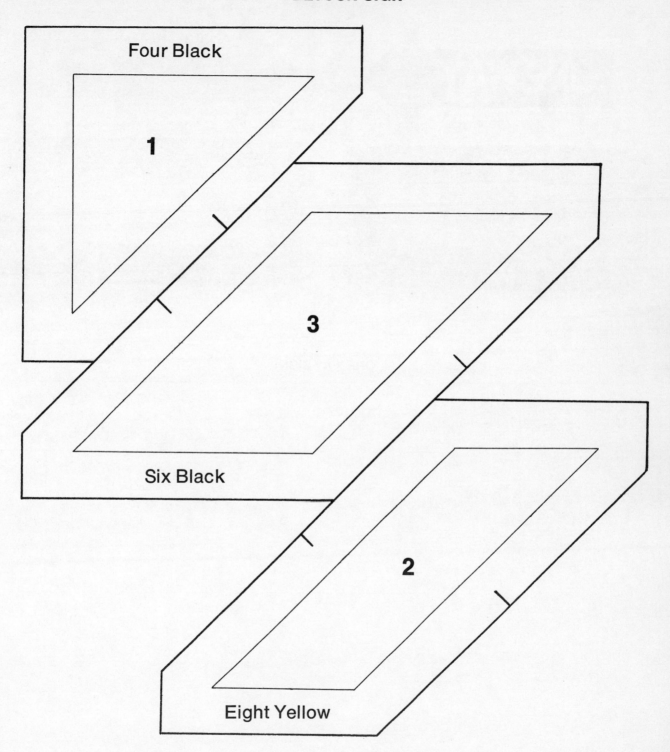

Four Black

**1**

**3**

Six Black

**2**

Eight Yellow

**ONE WAY SIGN**

| 2 | 5 | |
|---|---|---|
| 1 | 3 | 4 |
| 2 | 5 | |

## ONE WAY SIGN

Suggested Colors: White, Black

**White:**

> Cut one of Pattern 1
> Cut one of Pattern 3

**Black:**

> Cut two of Pattern 2
> Cut one of Pattern 4
> Cut two of Pattern 5

## STEP 1

> Sew a 2 on each side of 1, matching notches. Set aside to press later.
> Sew 3 to the end of 4.
> Sew a 5 on each side of 3-4 lengthwise.
> Press each piece.

## STEP 2

> Sew 2-1-2 to 3-4-5.
> Press.

Optional: Embroider ONE WAY in big block letters in white.

This pattern is also suitable in yellow and black without the letters. Just substitute black for white and yellow for black.

**ONE WAY SIGN**

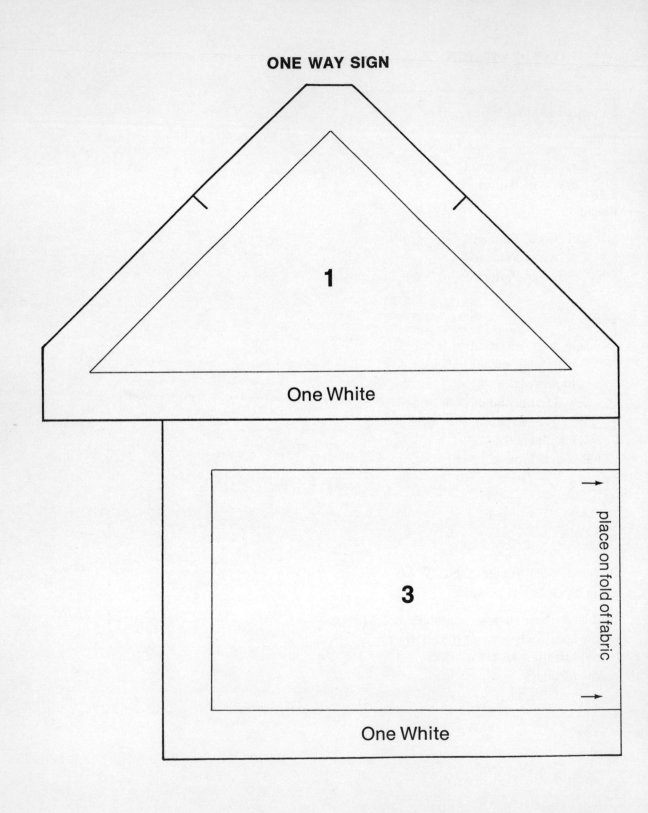

1

One White

3

place on fold of fabric

One White

# ONE WAY SIGN

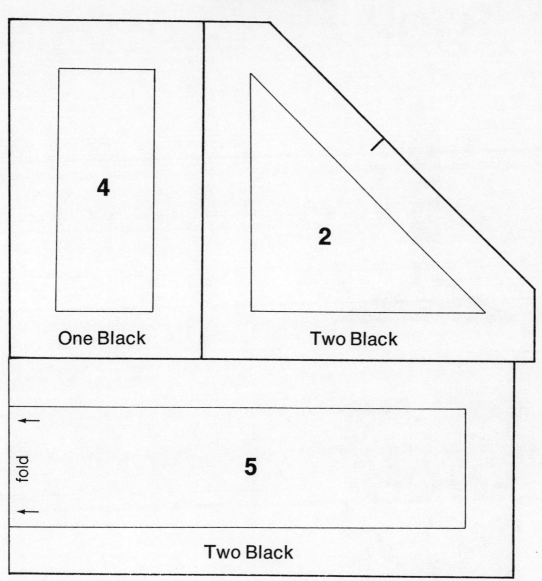

**4**

One Black

**2**

Two Black

fold

**5**

Two Black

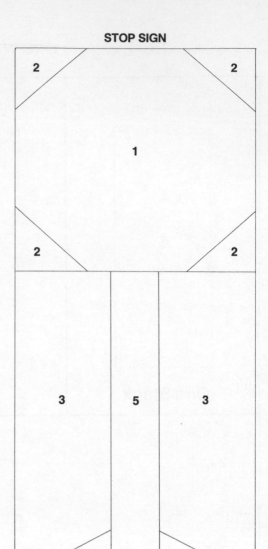

**STOP SIGN**

| 2 | | 2 |
|---|---|---|
| | 1 | |
| 2 | | 2 |
| 3 | 5 | 3 |
| | 4 | 4 |

## STOP SIGN

Suggested Colors: Red, Turquoise,
    Black

**Red:**

Cut one of Pattern 1

**Turquoise:**

Cut four of Pattern 2
Cut two of Pattern 3

**Black:**

Cut two of Pattern 4
Cut one of Pattern 5


## STEP 1

Sew a 2 piece to each corner of
    1, matching notches.
Sew 3 to 4, matching notches.
    Repeat.
Press each piece.

## STEP 2

Sew the 3-4 pieces on each side
    of 5, with the wider side of 4
    along 5 as in the diagram.
Press seams away from 5.

## STEP 3

Sew the sign (1-2) to the top of
    the stand (3-4-5).
Press on both sides.


Optional: Embroider STOP in big
white block letters on the red 1.

**STOP SIGN**

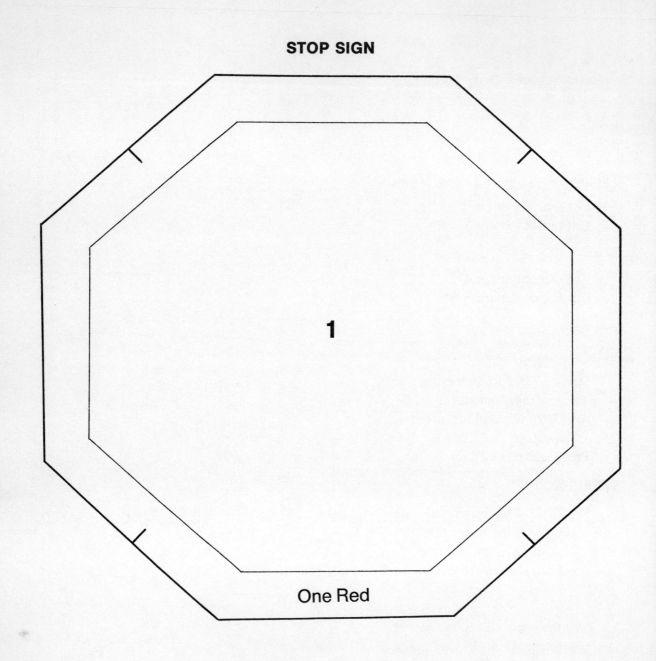

1

One Red

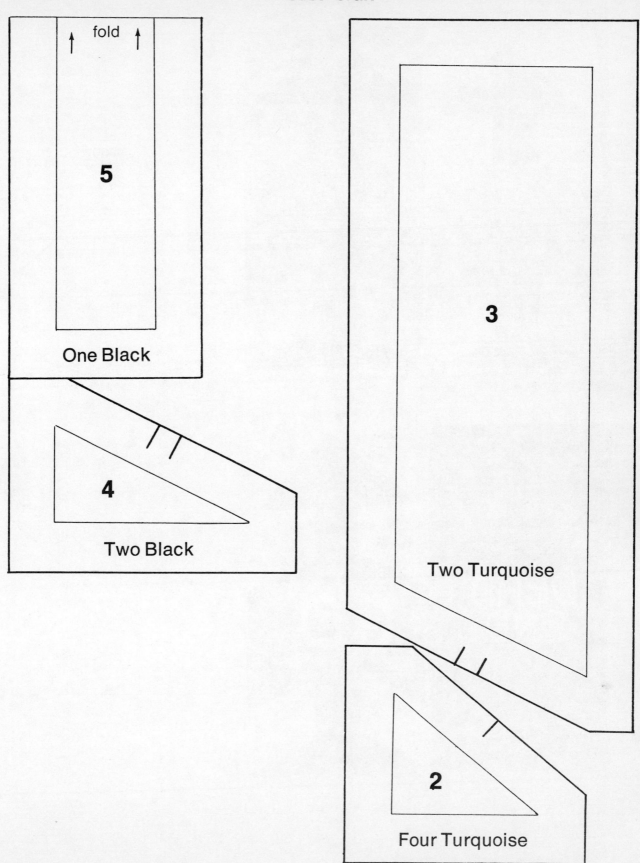

fold

5

One Black

4

Two Black

3

Two Turquoise

2

Four Turquoise

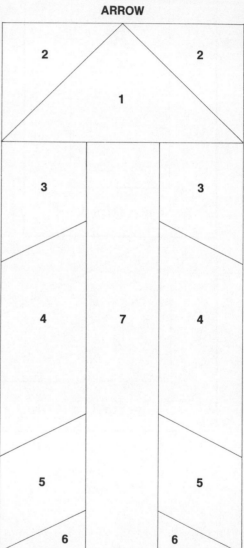

ARROW

## ARROW

Suggested Colors: Red, Turquoise

**Red:**

    Cut one of Pattern 1
    Cut two of Pattern 4
    Cut two of Pattern 6
    Cut one of Pattern 7

**Turquoise:**

    Cut two of Pattern 2
    Cut two of Pattern 3
    Cut two of Pattern 5

STEP 1

    Sew a 2 on each side of 1, matching notches.

    Sew 3, 4, 5, and 6 together in that order as indicated by the diagram, matching notches. Repeat.

STEP 2

    Sew 7 between both sections of 3-4-5-6, the wide side of 6 against 7 as in the diagram.

    Press.

STEP 3

    Sew the arrowhead (1-2) to the arrow (3-4-5-6-7).

    Give a final press on both sides.

Optional: Embroider various signs on each arrow you make: DEAD END, BUS STOP, ONE WAY, or PLAY STREET.

If you want to make a variety of arrows, you can save time by cutting several layers of cloth at once.

**ARROW**

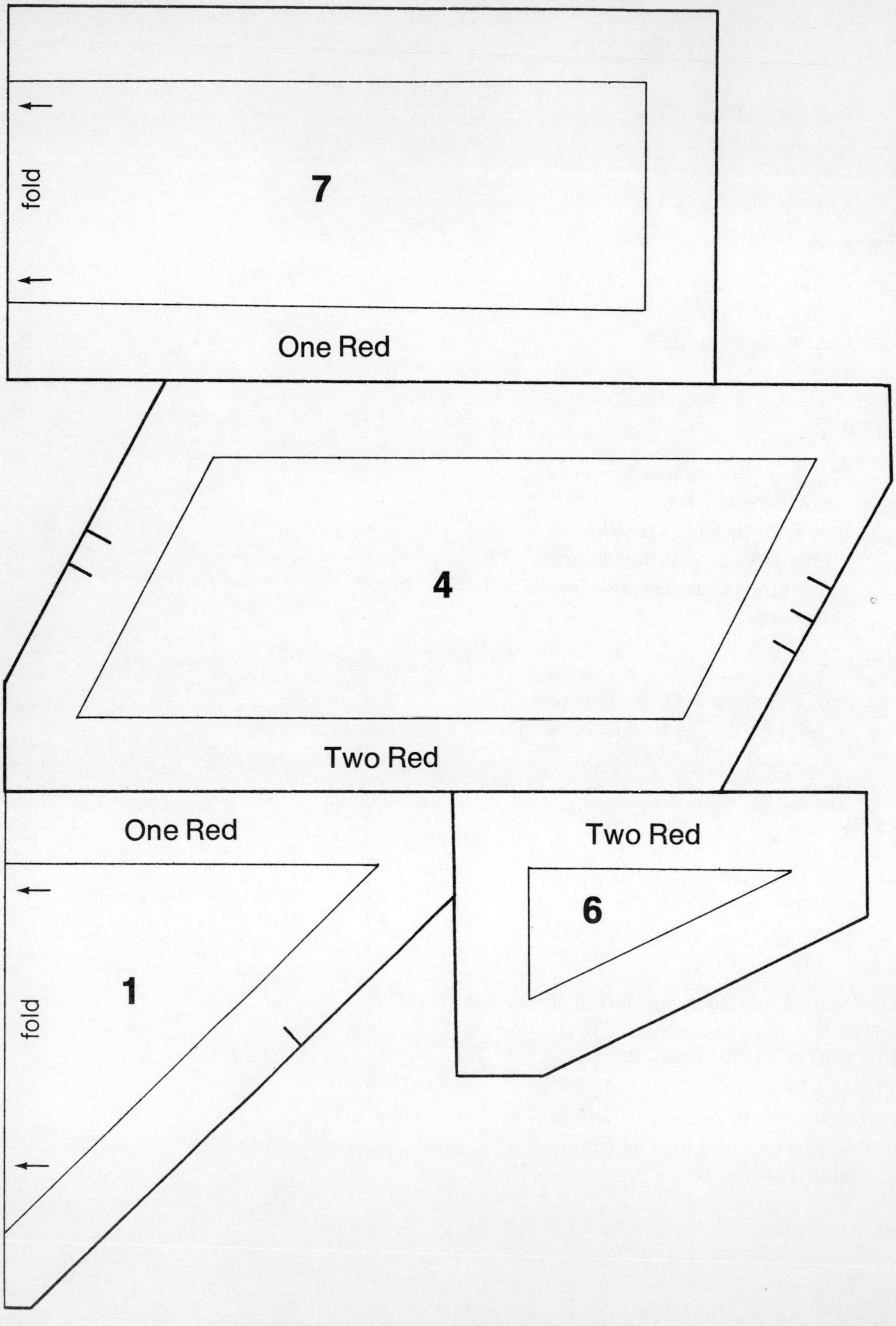

7

fold

One Red

4

Two Red

One Red

1

fold

Two Red

6

**ARROW**

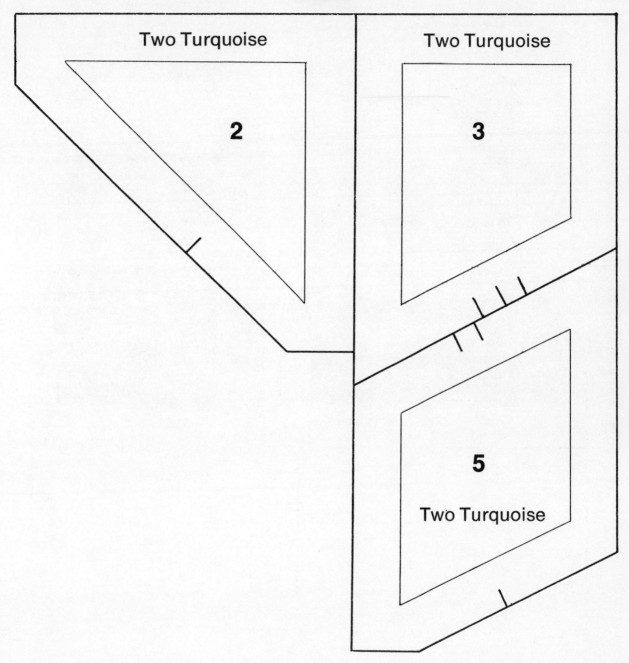

Two Turquoise

**2**

Two Turquoise

**3**

**5**

Two Turquoise

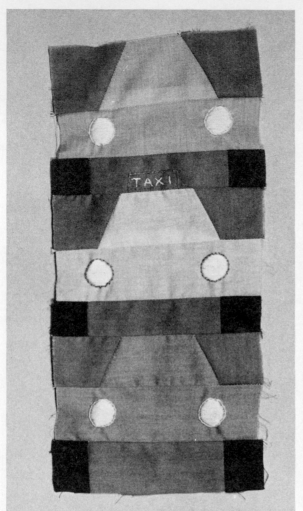

## CAR

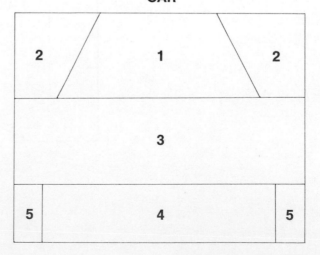

# CAR

Suggested Colors: Turquoise, Red and Five Other Colors, Black

**Turquoise:**

* Cut twelve of Pattern 2
Cut one of Pattern 4

**Red and Five Other Colors:**

Cut one of Pattern 1 from each color
Cut one of Pattern 3 from each color

**Black:**

Cut two of Pattern 5

* Cut 2 on fabric that has been folded in half, right side in, so both pieces will be facing opposite each other when opened out and right side up.
This pattern is designed to make six cars at one time; they are so easy to make, why not have a traffic jam?

## STEP 1

Sew the 2s on the sides of each of the six 1s as in the layout diagram, matching notches. Press seams away from 1.

## STEP 2

Sew a 3 on the bottom of each.

## STEP 3

Sew the two 5s on each side of 4.

Press and measure into six 2-inch sections and cut crosswise.

## STEP 4

Sew each one of these wheel sections on the bottom of each car.
Press.

Optional: Embroider headlights on each car and a TAXI sign on top of the yellow ones.

**CAR**

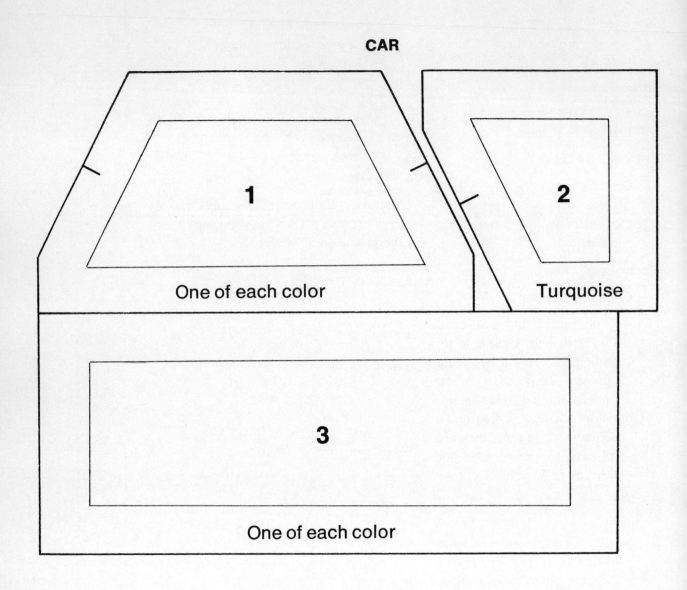

1

One of each color

2

Turquoise

3

One of each color

**CAR**

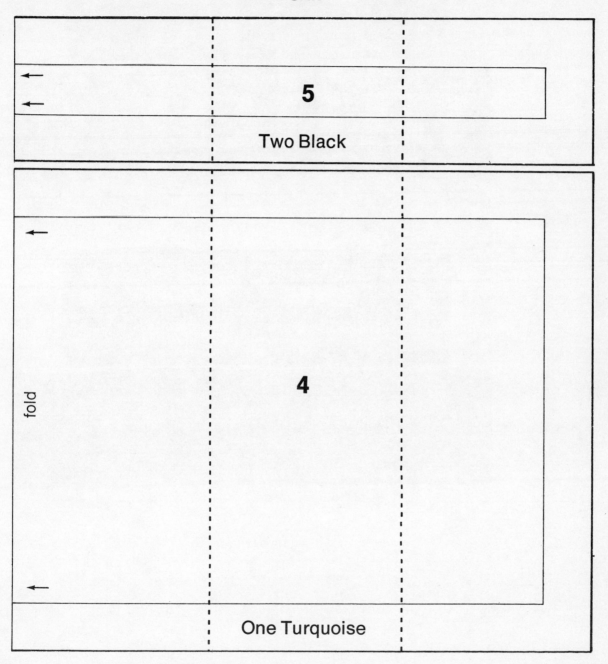

**5**

Two Black

fold

**4**

One Turquoise

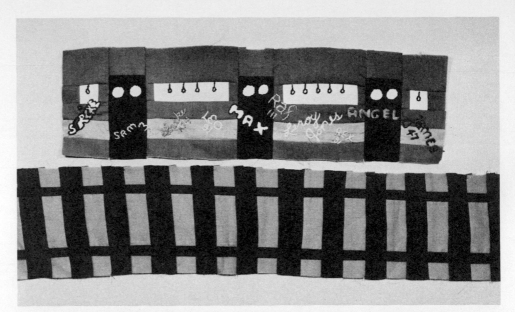

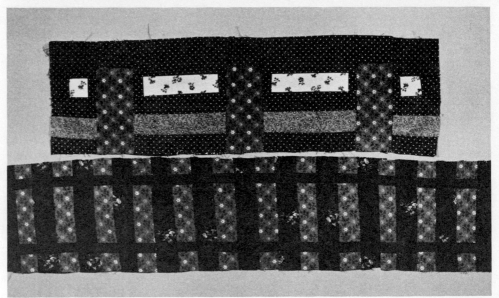

**SUBWAY CAR**

| 6 | | 2 | 9 | 2 | 9 | 2 | 6 | |
|---|---|---|---|---|---|---|---|---|
| 4 | 3 | 4 | 1 | 4 | 5 | 4 | 1 | 4 | 5 | 4 | 1 | 4 | 3 | 4 |
| 7 | | 10 | | 10 | | 7 |
| 7 | | 10 | | 10 | | 7 |
| 8 | | 11 | | 11 | | 8 |

# SUBWAY CAR

Suggested Colors: Green, Turquoise, White, Navy

## Green:

Cut three of Pattern 2
Cut eight of Pattern 4
Cut two of Pattern 6
Cut two of Pattern 7
Cut two of Pattern 8
Cut two of Pattern 9
Cut two of Pattern 10
Cut two of Pattern 11

## Turquoise:

Cut two of Pattern 7
Cut two of Pattern 10

## White:

Cut two of Pattern 3
Cut two of Pattern 5

## Navy:

Cut three of Pattern 1

Note: To avoid any confusion that may result from the fact that there are so many pieces, refer often to the diagram.

## STEP 1

Sew a 4 to both ends of each 3.
Sew a 4 to both ends of each 5.
Sew a turquoise 7 to each green 7.
Sew an 8 to each turquoise 7.
Sew a turquoise 10 to each green 10.
Sew 11 to each turquoise 10.
Press everything.

## STEP 2

Sew a 6 on top of each 4-3-4.
Sew 7-7-8 on the bottom of each 4-3-4.
Sew 9 on top of each 4-5-4.
Sew 10-10-11 on the bottom of each 4-5-4.
Press the four sections now completed.

## STEP 3

Sew a 2 on top of each of the three 1s.
Sew these three sections in between the four sections completed above in Step 2.
Press the completed subway car on the wrong side first.

Optional: Embroider graffiti on the subway car.

51

**SUBWAY CAR**

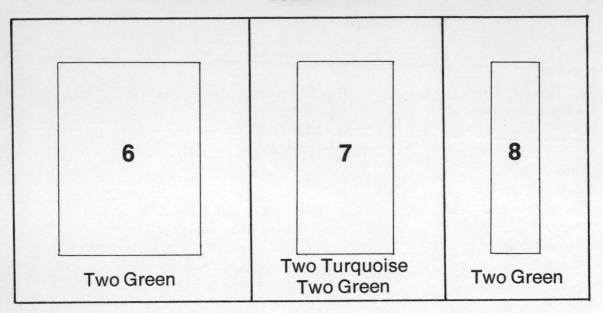

6
Two Green

7
Two Turquoise
Two Green

8
Two Green

1
Three Navy

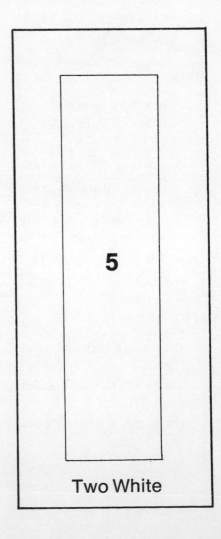

5
Two White

# SUBWAY CAR

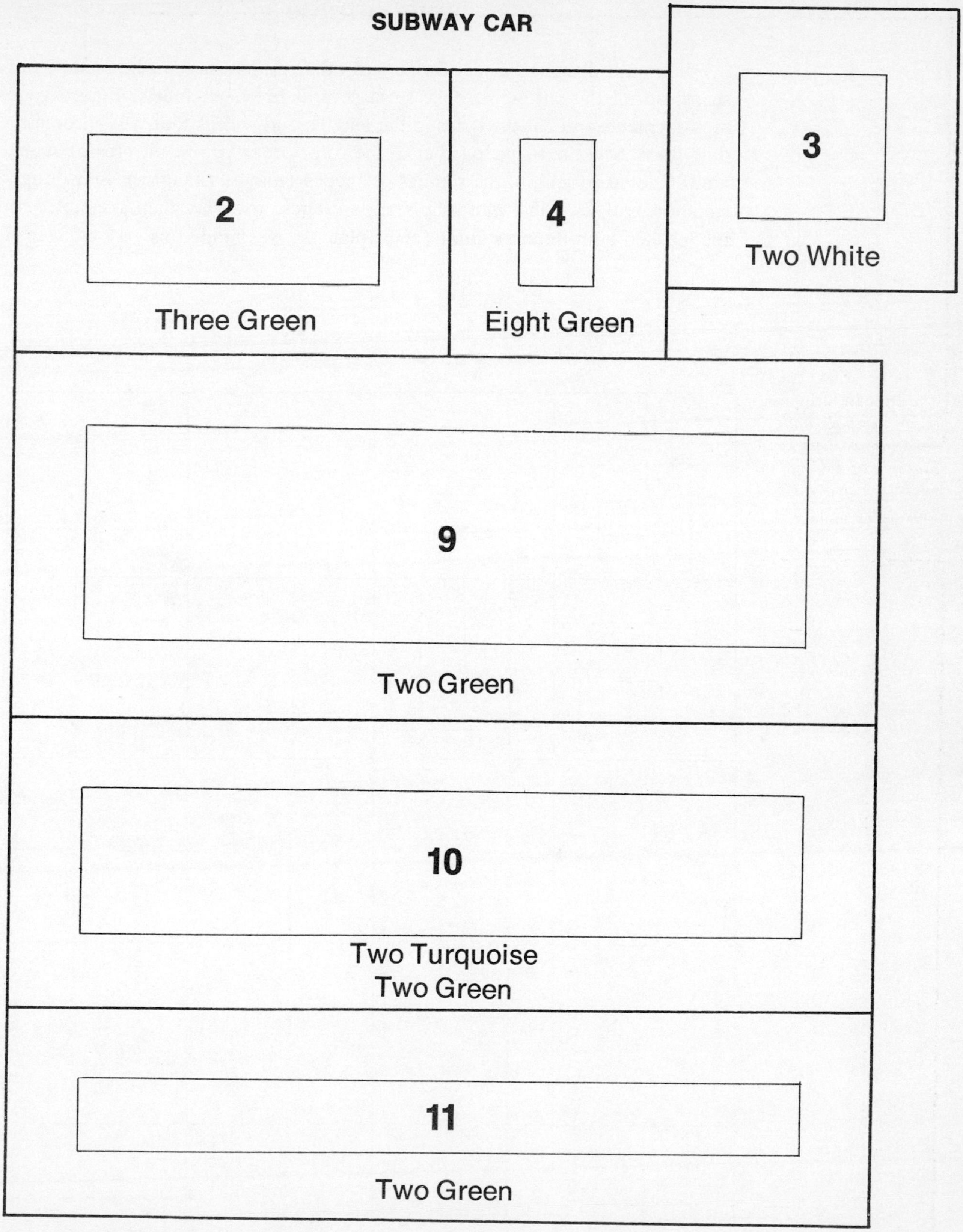

**2**

Three Green

**4**

Eight Green

**3**

Two White

**9**

Two Green

**10**

Two Turquoise
Two Green

**11**

Two Green

## STRIP METHOD

For a quilt like the Roman Stripe and other quilts that can be made from strips, do all the cutting at once from several layers of fabric. Figure your measurements and cut the strips in the lengths and widths that will accommodate them. Sew the strips together in the color order you want, press, cut the multi-colored strips into the squares or shapes (maybe triangles) your design calls for, and sew them into strip sections. These rows are then assembled as the finished quilt. Stuart's Quilt (color plate 7) was made this way.

*The* Roman Stripe *or* Jacob's Ladder *quilt diagrammed here is an example of a design in which the strip method can be used.*

## SUBWAY TRACKS

The Subway Tracks don't need a pattern. They are simply made from strips using the Strip Method.

For one yard of subway tracks that will serve as a separator in the finished quilt, cut three strips each of turquoise and navy that measure 2 by 36 inches —very quick and easy if you start with 36-inch-wide fabric. Place the two colors on top of each other, smooth the material out evenly, and pin the pieces together. With a yardstick mark off three rows 2 inches wide across the width of the fabric. Cut both layers as if they were one. You now have six strips, 2 by 36 inches, three turquoise and three navy.

Sew these six strips together lengthwise, alternating the colors as you go.

Press on the wrong side with the seams in one direction. Cut the piece neatly in half *across* the strips, and sew these two halves together side by side so the colors are still alternating.

Cut this piece into three equal 6-inch parts.

Sew these together side by side; you now have a row of tracks that measure 6 by 36 inches. For the rails, appliqué two rows of black seam binding by hand down the length of the tracks.

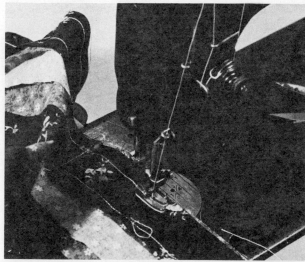

*Strips are sewn together lengthwise, alternating colors.*

*Below left:*
*Press the seams so that they are all turned in the same direction.*

*Below right:*
*Cut across the stripes, making each section six inches wide. The sections are then sewn together in a row.*

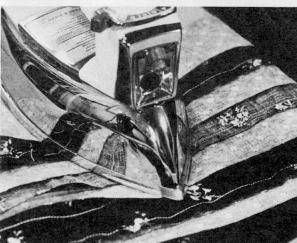

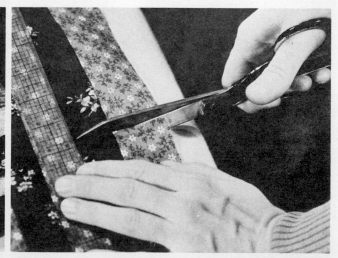

# WHEELS

There are two ways to make the wheels for all the vehicles in a "city quilt." The traditional way is to appliqué one layer of fabric to its background with the edges turned under. The method for impatient people, like me, is to sew two layers together and turn them right side out like a pillowcase. This method is faster and just as neat. The upper edge of the wheel is sewn into the seam above it and since the wheel is faced it can be left to hang free, creating a nice effect. This method was used for the scales of the fish pictured here. If you prefer, of course, the wheels can be hand sewn to the background.

Each wheel has a facing which is cut from the same pattern. After cutting, place each wheel right side down on its facing, and pin in place with one pin in the middle. Machine stitch around the curve, leaving the straight side open. Repeat for each wheel. Do all the wheels you will be using at once and don't bother to clip threads after each one. Just run the wheels one after the other through the machine, allowing about an inch of space between each, and clip when finished.

Trim the curves, turn the wheels right side out, pushing the curve out as much as possible, and press neatly.

Pin the wheels in place, at least ½ inch from each end of the background piece.

Place the upper part of the vehicle right side down on top of the wheel section and stitch the layers together, with the wheels between both layers.

Press the piece on the wrong side with the seam turned away from the wheels.

*The scales on this fish by Dianna James were my inspiration for the wheels in the city quilt designs.*

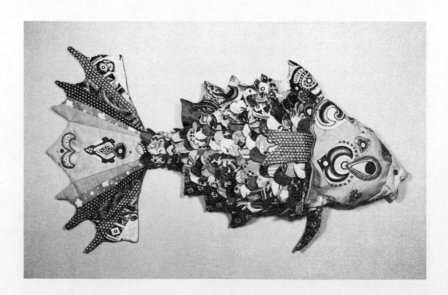

## CAR (Side View)

| | | 6 | | |
|---|---|---|---|---|
| 2 | | 1 | | 3 |
| | | 4 | | |
| 7 | | 5 | | 7 |

Suggested Colors: Turquoise, Black, Red and Five Other Colors

**Turquoise:**

Cut six of Pattern 2
Cut six of Pattern 3
Cut six of Pattern 5
Cut six of Pattern 6

**Black:**

Cut twelve of Pattern 7 (plus twelve facings)

**Red and Five Other Colors:**

Cut one of Pattern 1 from each color
Cut one of Pattern 4 from each color

These instructions are for making six cars at a time.

For cutting, simply place six colors one on top of the other and cut as one layer.

STEP 1

Sew 1 between 2 and 3, matching notches. Press seams out.

STEP 2

Sew 6 on top of 2-1-3.
Sew 4 on the bottom of 2-1-3.
Sew the wheels (7) as instructed previously and press along with the car body.

STEP 3

Pin the wheels on 5 in the appropriate places (at least ½ inch from the ends of 5).
Place the car body face down on 5 and sew.
Press the finished car.

Optional: Cars can be made two-toned by switching the top and bottom colors.

## CAR (Side View)

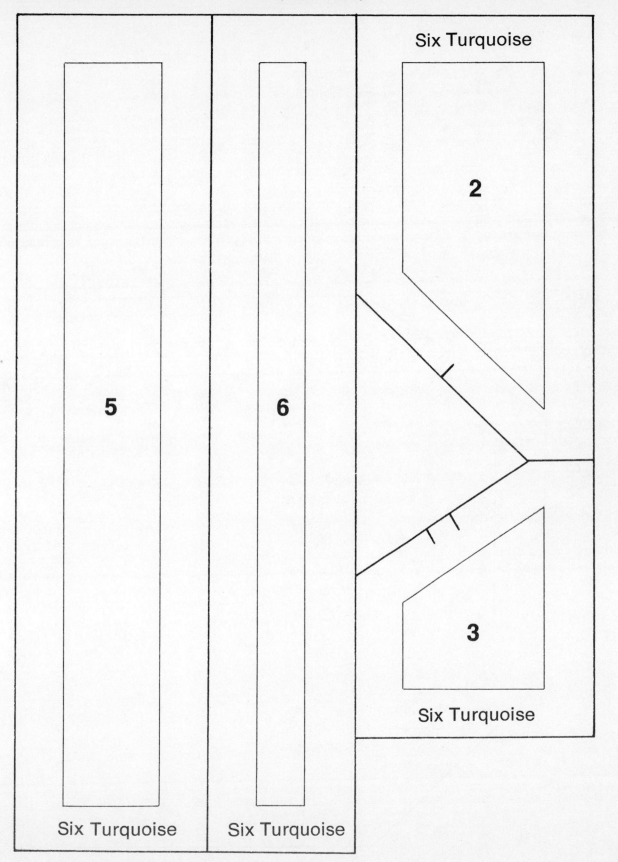

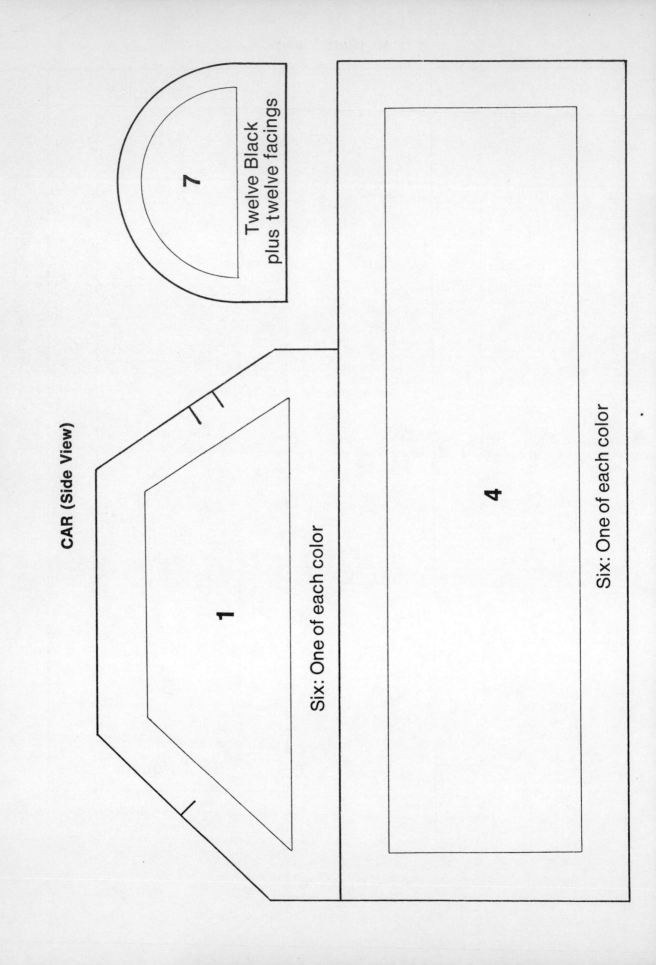

CAR (Side View)

**7**

Twelve Black
plus twelve facings

**1**

Six: One of each color

**4**

Six: One of each color

## MAIL TRUCK

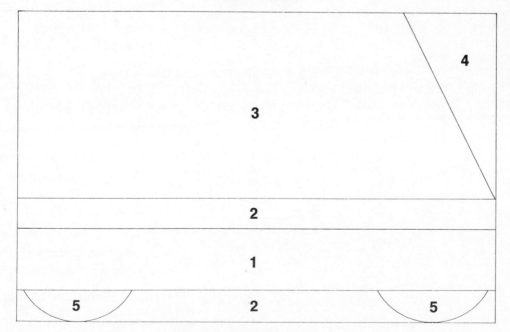

Suggested Colors: Turquoise, Black, White, Red, Navy

**Turquoise:**

Cut one of Pattern 2
Cut one of Pattern 4

**Black:**

Cut two of Pattern 5 (plus two facings)

**White:**

Cut one of Pattern 3

**Red:**

Cut one of Pattern 2

**Navy:**

Cut one of Pattern 1

STEP 1

Sew 1, the red 2, 3, and 4 together in that order, matching the notches on 3 and 4.
Sew the wheels (5) as instructed previously and press the wheels and truck body.

STEP 2

Pin the wheels to the turquoise 2 in the appropriate places (at least ½ inch from the ends).
Place the mail truck body face down on 2 and sew.
Press the finished piece.

Optional: Embroider MAIL on the side in red

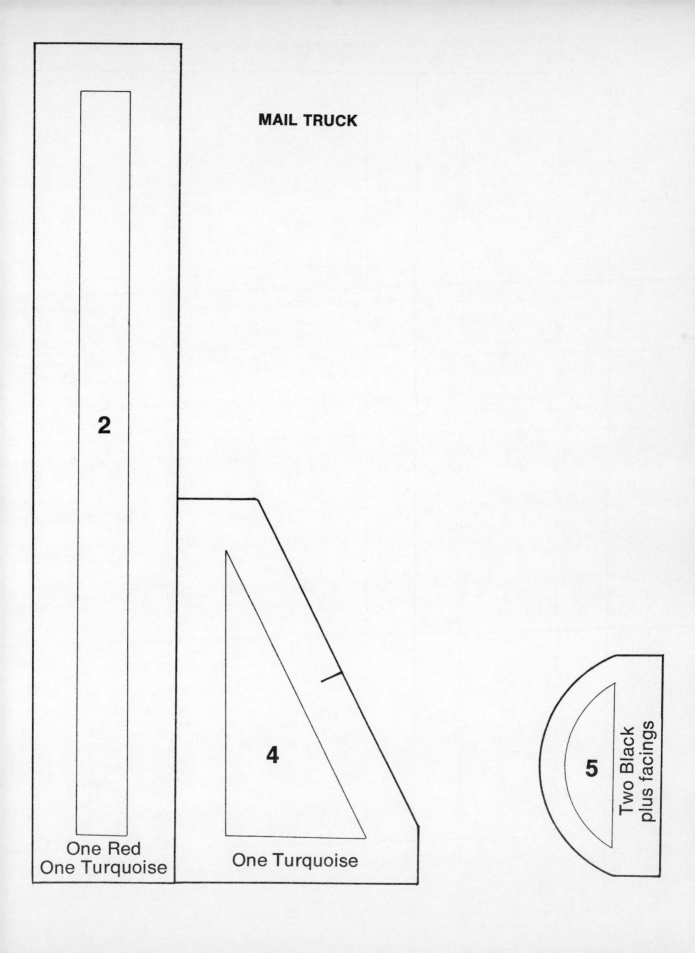

**MAIL TRUCK**

**2**

One Red
One Turquoise

**4**

One Turquoise

**5**

Two Black
plus facings

# MAIL TRUCK

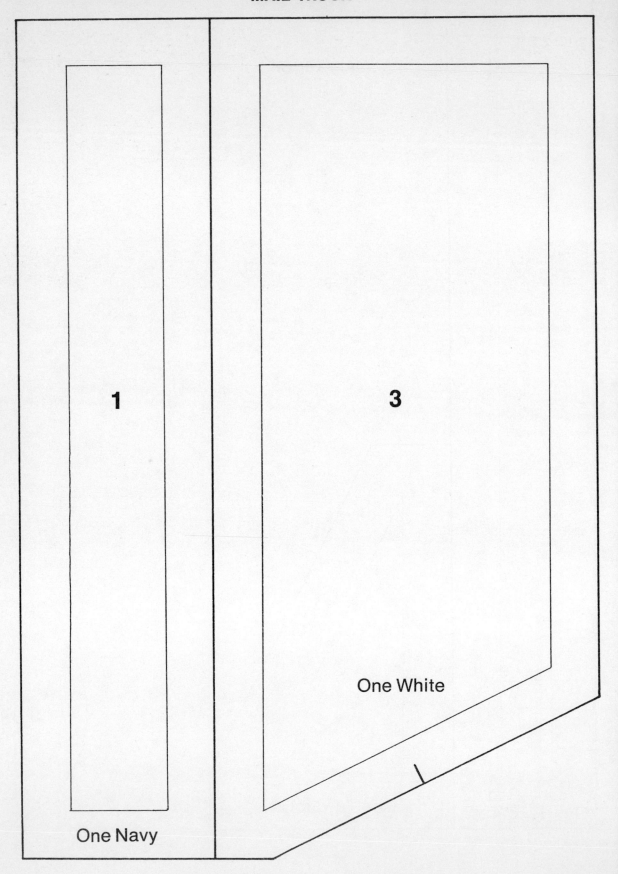

**1**

**3**

One White

One Navy

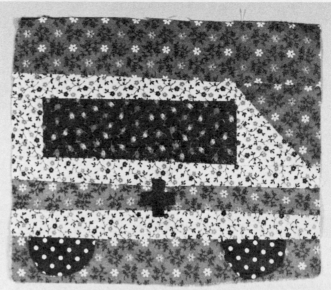

## AMBULANCE

| | | 2 | | |
|---|---|---|---|---|
| | | 5 | | 6 |
| 4 | | 3 | 6 | |
| | | 2 | | |
| | | 2 | | |
| | | 2 | | |
| 7 | | 1 | 7 | |

Suggested Colors: Turquoise, White, Red, Black

**Turquoise:**

Cut one of Pattern 1
Cut one of Pattern 2
Cut one of Pattern 3
Cut one of Pattern 6

**White:**

Cut two of Pattern 2
Cut one of Pattern 4
Cut one of Pattern 5
Cut one of Pattern 6

**Red:**

Cut one of Pattern 2

**Black:**

Cut two of Pattern 7 (plus two facings)

## STEP 1

Sew two white 2s to top and bottom of red 2 (check diagram).
Sew white 6 to turquoise 6, matching notches.
Sew 3 to 4, checking diagram.
Make wheels according to instructions on p. 56 and press all pieces.

## STEP 2

Sew 5 to the top of 3-4 (with 4 to the left of 3).
Press seam toward turquoise.

## STEP 3

Sew the white 6 to the right of 3-4-5.
Press.

## STEP 4

Sew the turquoise 2 on top of the ambulance.
Sew the red and white 2 section to the bottom.
Pin the wheels (7) to 1 in the appropriate places along the straight edge, at least ½ inch from the ends.
Place the ambulance body face down on 1 and sew lengthwise.
Press.

Optional: Embroider a red light on top and a red cross on the side.

**AMBULANCE**

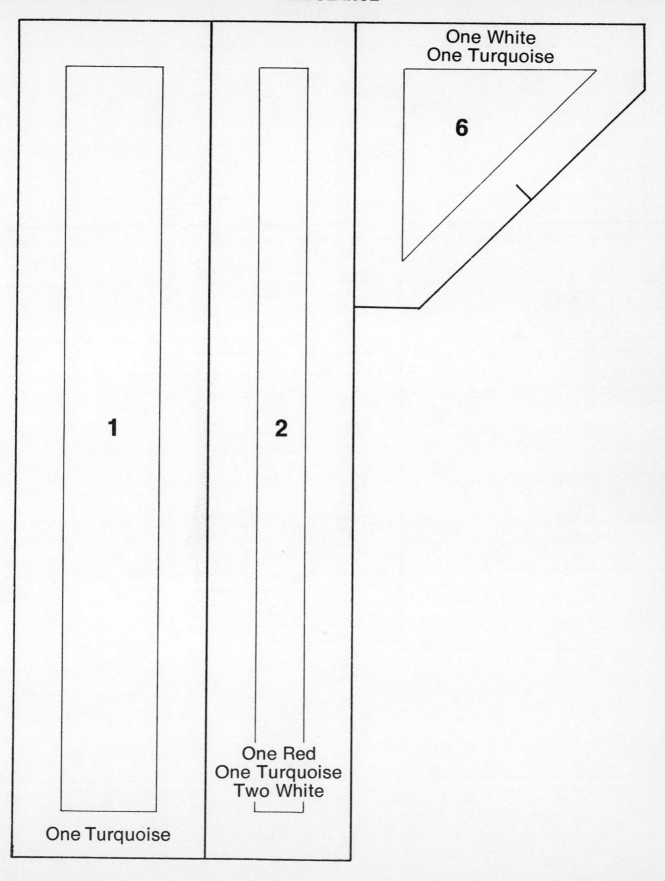

One White
One Turquoise

6

1

2

One Red
One Turquoise
Two White

One Turquoise

# AMBULANCE

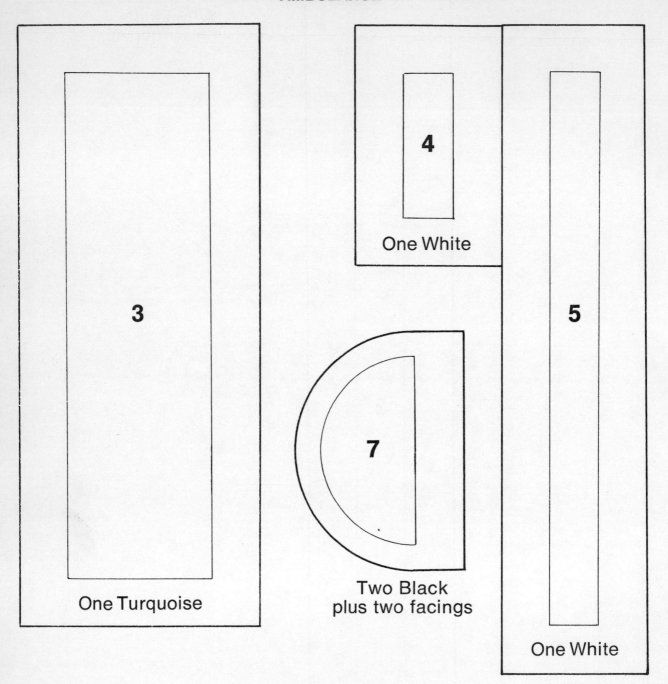

**3**
One Turquoise

**4**
One White

**7**
Two Black
plus two facings

**5**
One White

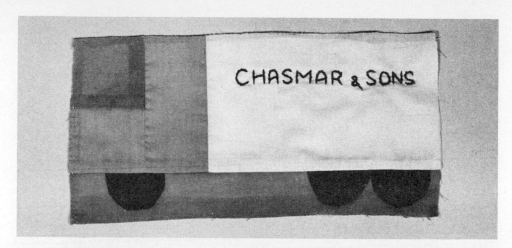

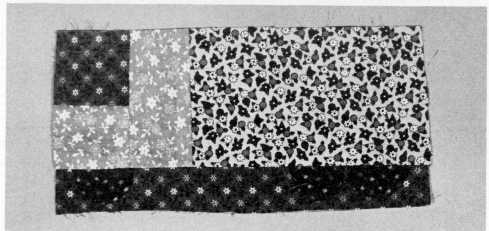

## TRAILER TRUCK

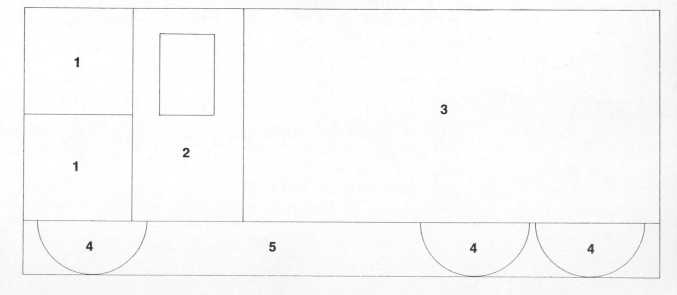

Suggested Colors: Red, Yellow, Black, Turquoise

**Red:**

Cut one of Pattern 1
Cut one of Pattern 2

**Yellow:**

Cut one of Pattern 3

**Black:**

Cut three of Pattern 4 (plus three facings)

**Turquoise:**

Cut one of Pattern 1
* Cut one of Pattern 5
Cut one of Pattern 2 for facing if you want a window in the cab.

* 5 is cut on the fold of the fabric.

STEP 1

Sew the red 1 to the turquoise 1.
Sew 2 to the right side of 1-1.
Sew 3 to the right side of 2.
Make the wheels (4) and press, pressing the other pieces at the same time.

STEP 2

Pin the wheels to 5 in the appropriate place (at least ½ inch from either end) along the straight edge of each wheel.

Place the bottom side of the trailer truck face down on 5 and sew.
Press on the wrong side with the seam toward the truck.
Give the piece a final press on the right side.

Optional: Embroider the name of a trucking company or of your family on the side.

If you want the trailer truck to head in the opposite direction, sew 2 to the left side of 1-1 and 3 to the left side of 2.

If you want the cab of the trailer truck to have a window, cut an X along the dotted line indicated on pattern piece 2, fold the edges under, pin in place on a piece of turquoise also cut from 2, and hem stitch by hand all around the sewing line that marks the window. Treat both as one piece and continue with Step 1.

# TRAILER TRUCK

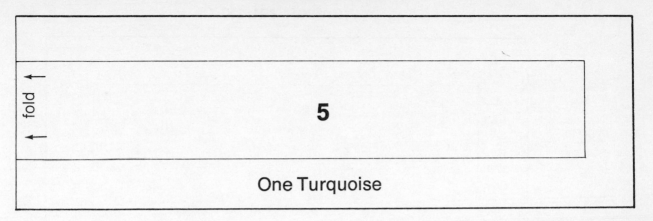

**5**

One Turquoise

fold

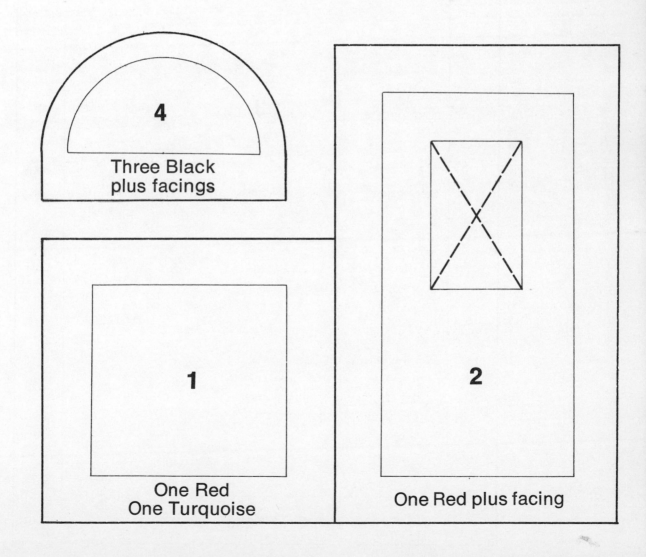

**4**

Three Black
plus facings

**1**

One Red
One Turquoise

**2**

One Red plus facing

# TRAILER TRUCK

**3**

One Yellow

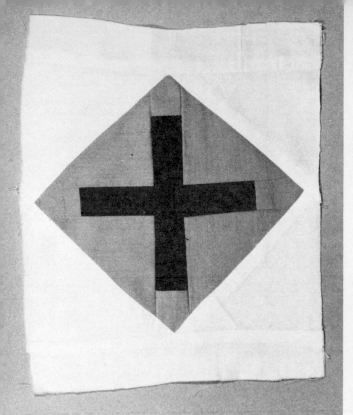

**INTERSECTION**

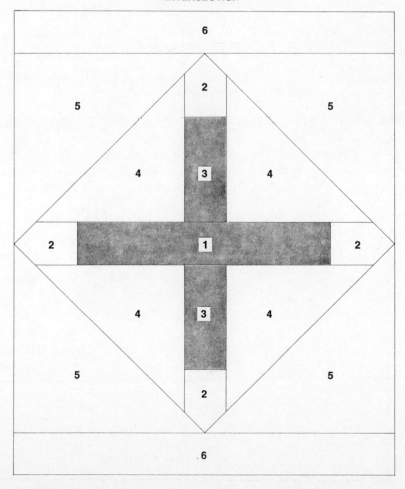

# INTERSECTION

Suggested Colors: Black, Yellow, White

**Black:**

    Cut one of Pattern 1
    Cut two of Pattern 3

**Yellow:**

    Cut four of Pattern 2
    Cut four of Pattern 4

**White:**

    Cut four of Pattern 5
    Cut two of Pattern 6

STEP 1

    Sew 2 on the end of each 3 and on each end of 1.
    Press seams toward black.

STEP 2

    Sew a 4 to the right and left sides of each 2-3.
    Press seams toward black.

STEP 3

    Sew 2-1-2 between the two 2-3-4 pieces, checking diagram.
    Press.

STEP 4

    Sew a 5 to each 4, matching notches.
    Press seams out.

STEP 5

    Sew a 6 on the top and bottom of the square.
    Press the finished sign.

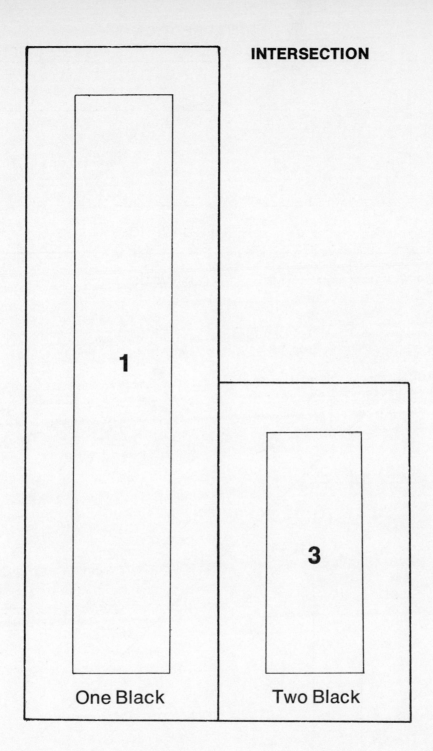

**1**

**3**

One Black

Two Black

# INTERSECTION

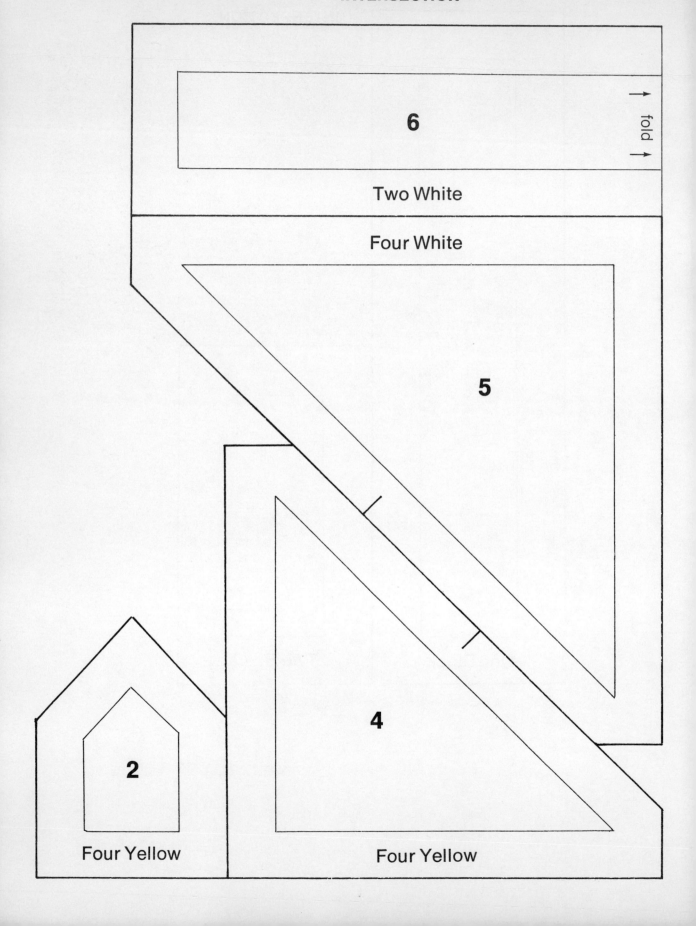

6

fold

Two White

Four White

5

4

2

Four Yellow

Four Yellow

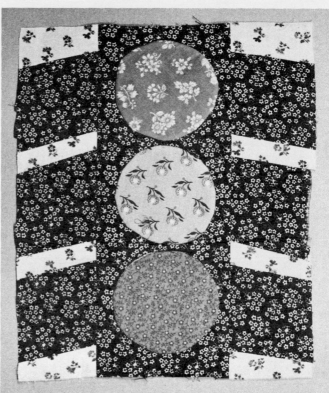

**TRAFFIC LIGHT**

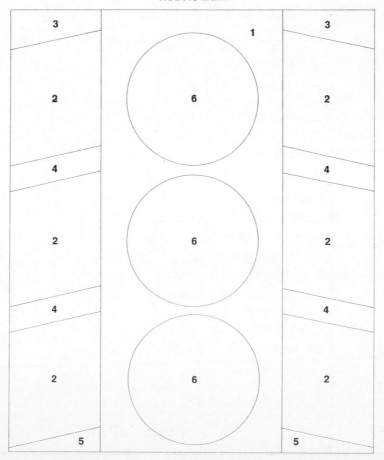

# TRAFFIC LIGHT

Suggested Colors: Green, White, Red, Yellow, Light Green

For Pattern 1 simply measure and cut a piece 5½ by 12 inches.

Cut Patterns 2, 3, 4, and 5 from one piece of fabric folded in half with right side in.

**Green:**

Cut one of Pattern 1
Cut six of Pattern 2

**White:**

Cut two of Pattern 3
Cut four of Pattern 4
Cut two of Pattern 5

**Red, Yellow, Light Green:**

Cut one of Pattern 6 from each color (plus facings for each one)

STEP 1

Sew all the 2, 3, 4, and 5 pieces together in the order indicated by the diagram, matching all the notches.
Repeat for the other side.
Place each 6 face down on its facing, pin and sew a ¼-inch seam all the way around. Slash the facing and turn each circle right side out through the slash and press neatly.
Press the other pieces at the same time.

STEP 2

Sew a 2-3-4-5 section to each side of 1 and press.

STEP 3

Pin the three 6 circles (red, yellow, and green) down the middle of 1 and sew them by hand with very small hemming stitches.
Press.

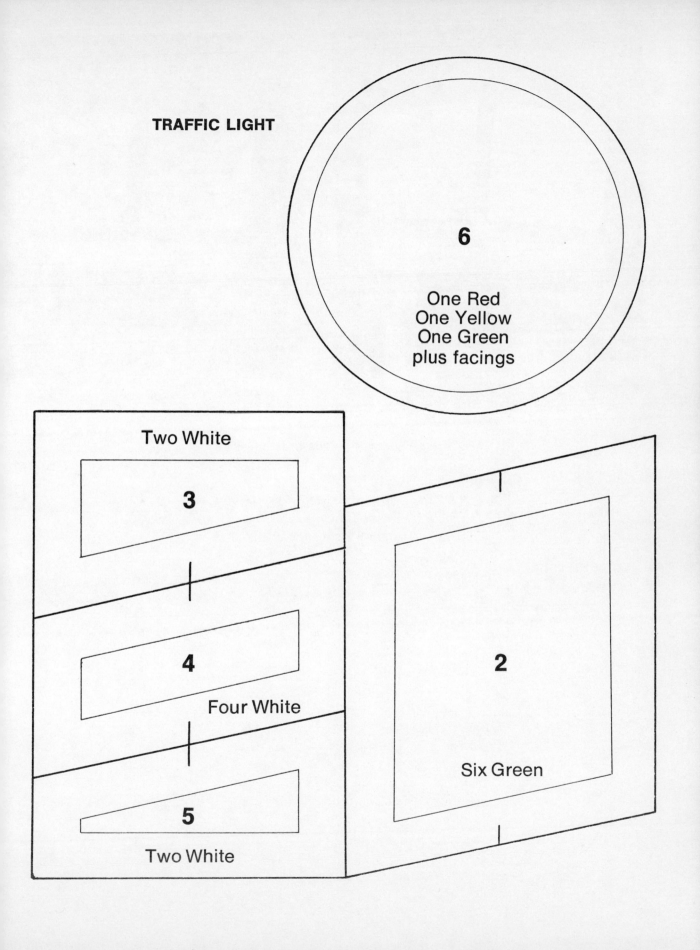

**TRAFFIC LIGHT**

6

One Red
One Yellow
One Green
plus facings

Two White

3

4

Four White

5

Two White

2

Six Green

 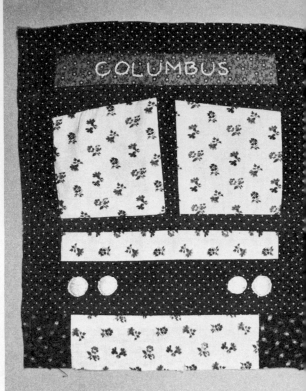

**BUS**

| | | | | |
|---|---|---|---|---|
| | | 3 | | |
| 2 | | 1 | | 2 |
| | 6 | | 6 | |
| 5 | 4 | 7 | 4 | 5 |
| | | 3 | | |
| 2 | | 1 | | 2 |
| | | 8 | | |
| 10 | | 9 | | 10 |

# BUS

Suggested Colors: Green, Turquoise, White, Black

**Green:**

Cut four of Pattern 2
* Cut two of Pattern 3
Cut two of Pattern 5
Cut two of Pattern 6
Cut one of Pattern 7
* Cut one of Pattern 8

**Turquoise:**

Cut one of Pattern 1

**White:**

Cut one of Pattern 1
Cut two of Pattern 4
* Cut one of Pattern 9

**Black:**

Cut two of Pattern 10

* 3, 8, and 9 are drawn for cutting on the fold

## STEP 1

Sew a 2 on each side of the turquoise 1, matching notches.
Sew a 2 on each side of the white 1.
Sew a 4 to each 5, matching notches.
Sew a 10 to each side of 9, matching notches.
Press everything completed above, with seams facing away from white.

## STEP 2

Sew 3 on top of each 1-2.
Sew 6 on top of each 4-5, checking diagram.
Sew 8 on the bottom of the white group of 1-2.
Sew 9-10 on the bottom of 8.
Press everything completed above.

## STEP 3

Sew 7 between the two groups of 4-5-6, checking diagram.
Press seams away from 7.

## STEP 4

Sew the turquoise group of 1-2-3 on top of 4-5-6-7.
Sew this to the bottom half of the bus.
Press the finished bus on the wrong side first, then on the right side.

Optional: Embroider the number and destination of your local bus on the turquoise 1, and yellow headlights on 8.

## BUS

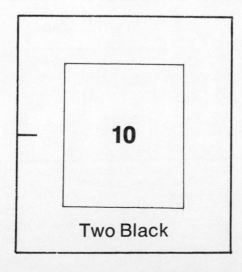

10

Two Black

**BUS**

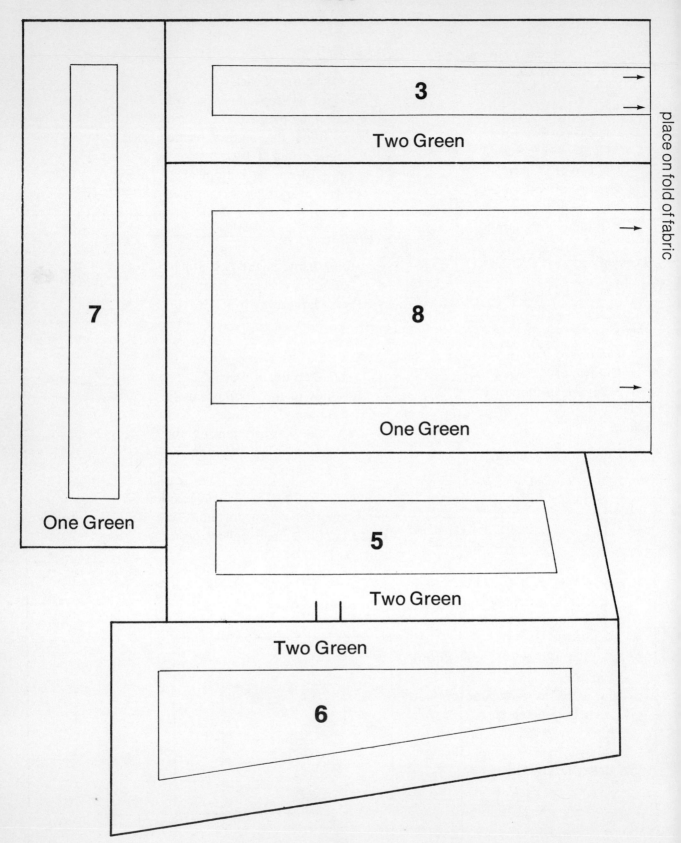

place on fold of fabric

**3**

Two Green

**8**

One Green

**7**

One Green

**5**

Two Green

Two Green

**6**

**BUS**

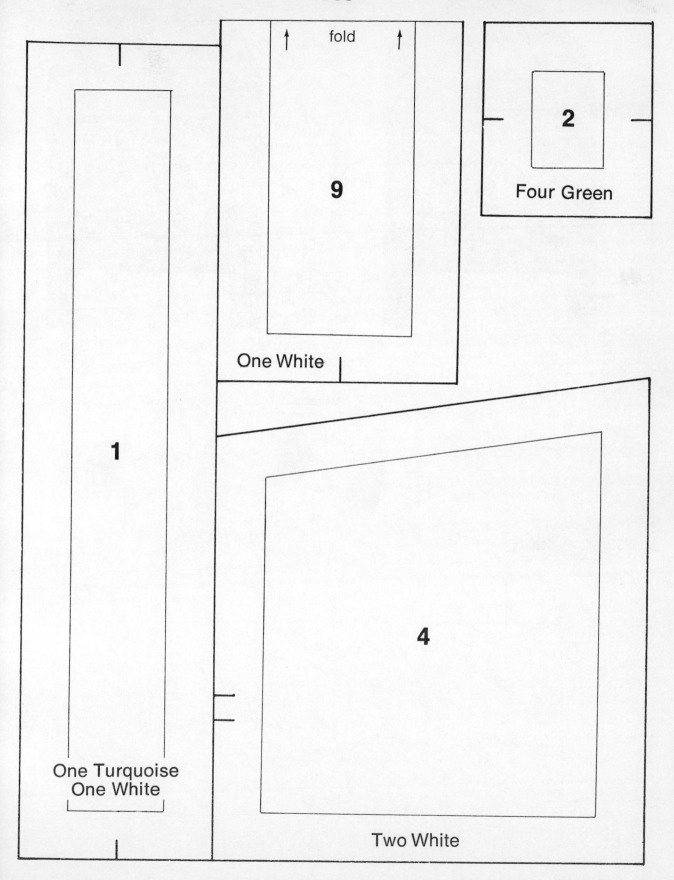

fold

9

One White

2

Four Green

1

One Turquoise
One White

4

Two White

**MAILBOX**

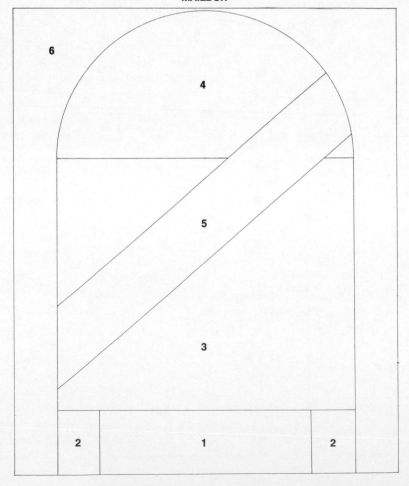

# MAILBOX

Suggested Colors: White, Blue, Red

**White:**

Cut one of Pattern 1
Cut one 10- by 12-inch block (number 6 on pattern layout diagram)

**Blue:**

Cut two of Pattern 2
Cut one of Pattern 3
Cut one of Pattern 4

**Red:**

Cut one 2½- by 11-inch strip (number 5 on pattern layout diagram)

STEP 1

Sew a 2 on each end of 1.
Sew 3 to 4.
Press both pieces. At the same time press a ½-inch seam allowance on both sides of 5.

STEP 2

Sew 1-2 to 3-4.
Place 5 diagonally across the mailbox until you are satisfied with its position. Pin it down and hand sew both edges down with tiny hem stitches.
Press.

STEP 3

Place the mailbox face down on facing material and cut out a matching facing. Pin together and sew a ½-inch seam around, leaving the straight side open. Trim the seam allowance and turn the mailbox right side out through the open end.
Press neatly.

STEP 4

Place the mailbox on top of 6 and center so the bottom edge matches the bottom edge of 6. Pin in place and hand sew all around the outside edge of the mailbox with tiny hem stitches.
Give the block a final press on its right side.

Optional: Embroider MAILBOX in block letters with a chain stitch in white.

85

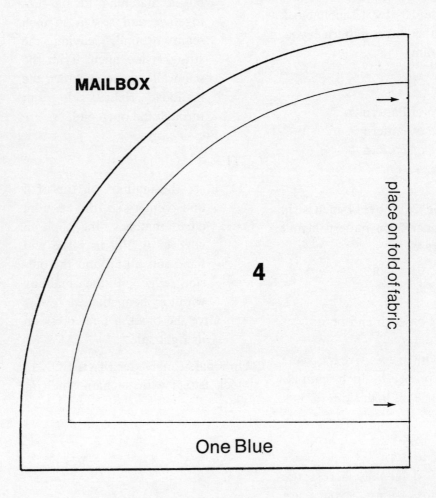

**MAILBOX**

4

place on fold of fabric

One Blue

# MAILBOX

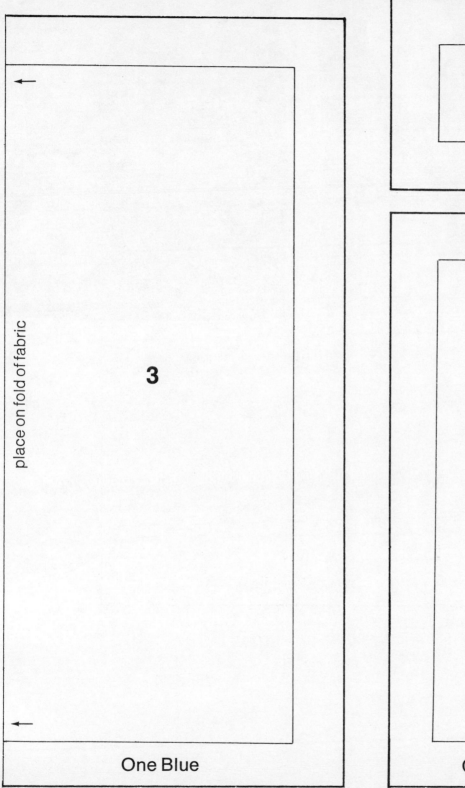

place on fold of fabric

**3**

One Blue

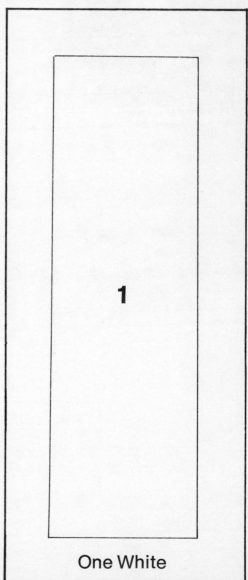

**2**

Two Blue

**1**

One White

**1976**

# 1976

To change the date, make other numbers following the patternmaking instructions given earlier.

This block is divided into four parts, one for each letter.

To make numbers in the same color:

## STEP 1

Cut out two 10- by 12-inch blocks in the colors you've chosen. Press the one to be used as the background color in half lengthwise and crosswise, dividing it into four parts. These creases act as a guide for tracing the patterns.

Trace the *sewing line* of each number with a pencil or a marking pen.

## STEP 2

Using a small stitch, machine stitch a line right on top of the line just traced. Repeat for each number.

Cut out the middle of each number leaving a ¼-inch seam allowance on the inside of the stitching line.

Clip the corners to the stitching line.

## STEP 3

Pin this piece down on the other piece of contrasting color, matching up the corners.

Turn the edges of the numbers and pin them to the piece underneath.

Using a tiny hem stitch, hand sew around the edges of each number.

Press on right side.

For different-colored backgrounds or numbers, cut separate blocks in the desired colors, using the patterns given.

**1976**

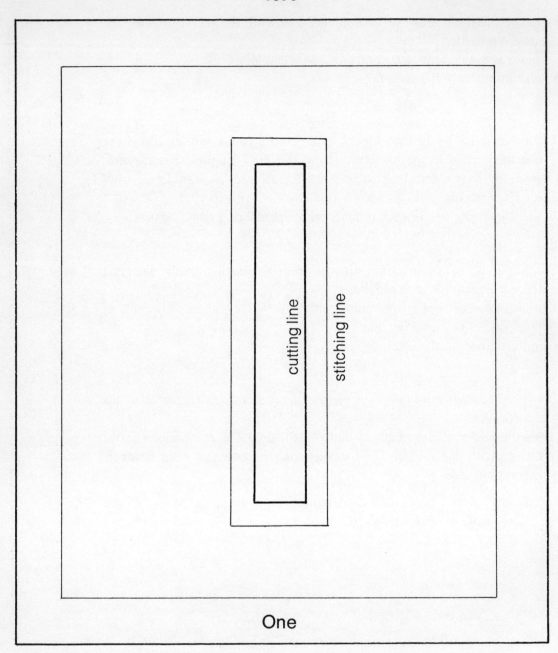

cutting line

stitching line

One

**1976**

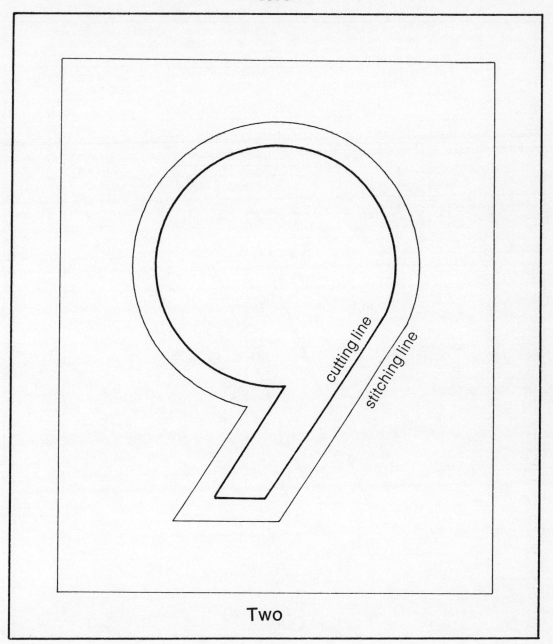

cutting line

stitching line

Two

**1976**

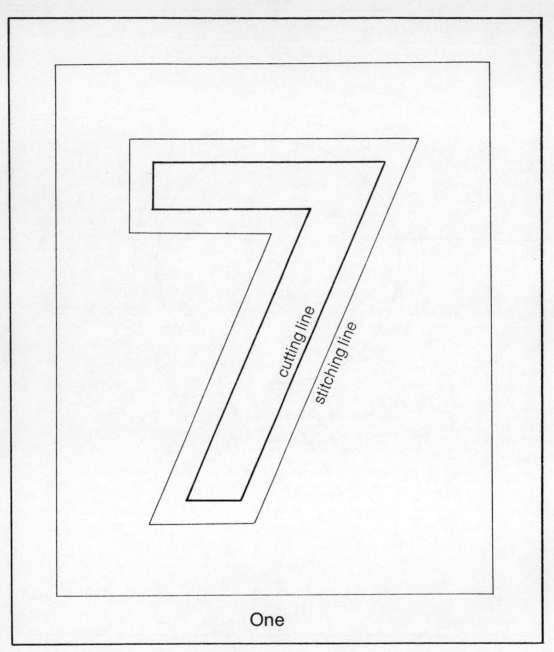

cutting line

stitching line

One

**HOT DOG WAGON**

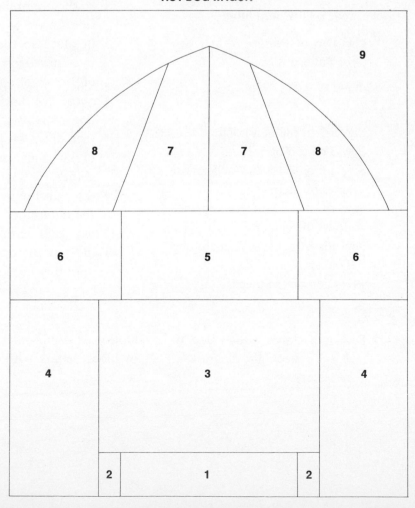

Suggested Colors: White, Orange, Black

To make Pattern 9 measure a block 5½ by 10 inches.

## White:

Cut one of Pattern 1
Cut two of Pattern 4
Cut two of Pattern 6
Cut one of Pattern 9

## Orange:

Cut one of Pattern 3
Cut one of Pattern 5

## Black:

Cut two of Pattern 2

## green, red, yellow, and blue:

Cut two of Pattern 7 and two of Pattern 8

## STEP 1

Sew a 2 to each end of 1.
Sew 3 on top of 1-2.
Sew a 6 on each end of 5 (short sides of each).
Sew the two 7 pieces together down the center.
Sew an 8 to each 7, matching notches.
Press completed pieces.

## STEP 2

Sew a 4 down either side of 1-2-3, checking diagram if necessary.

Press seams out. Press 7-8 at the same time.

Lay 7-8 face down on plain fabric that can be used as a facing. Pin in place and cut facing, using 7-8 as the pattern.

Stitch the umbrella (7-8) to the facing ½ inch around the curve, leaving the straight side open. Trim the curve. Turn the umbrella right side out through this opening.

Press neatly.

## STEP 3

Sew 5-6 to the top of 1-2-3-4.

Lay the umbrella (7-8) right side up on top of 9 and pin in place so the bottom edge is centered on the long side of 9.

Lay the bottom half of the hot dog wagon (1-2-3-4-5-6) face down on top of the umbrella half and stitch together.

Press with the seam away from the umbrella.

Press again on the right side.

Hand sew the edge of 7-8 to 9 with tiny hem stitches.

Optional: Embroider HOT DOGS in block letters with a chain stitch on 3.

**HOT DOG WAGON**

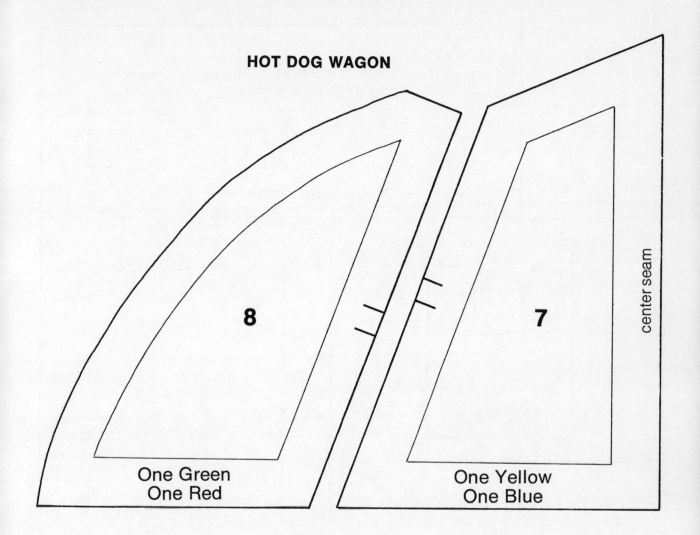

8

One Green
One Red

7

One Yellow
One Blue

center seam

# HOT DOG WAGON

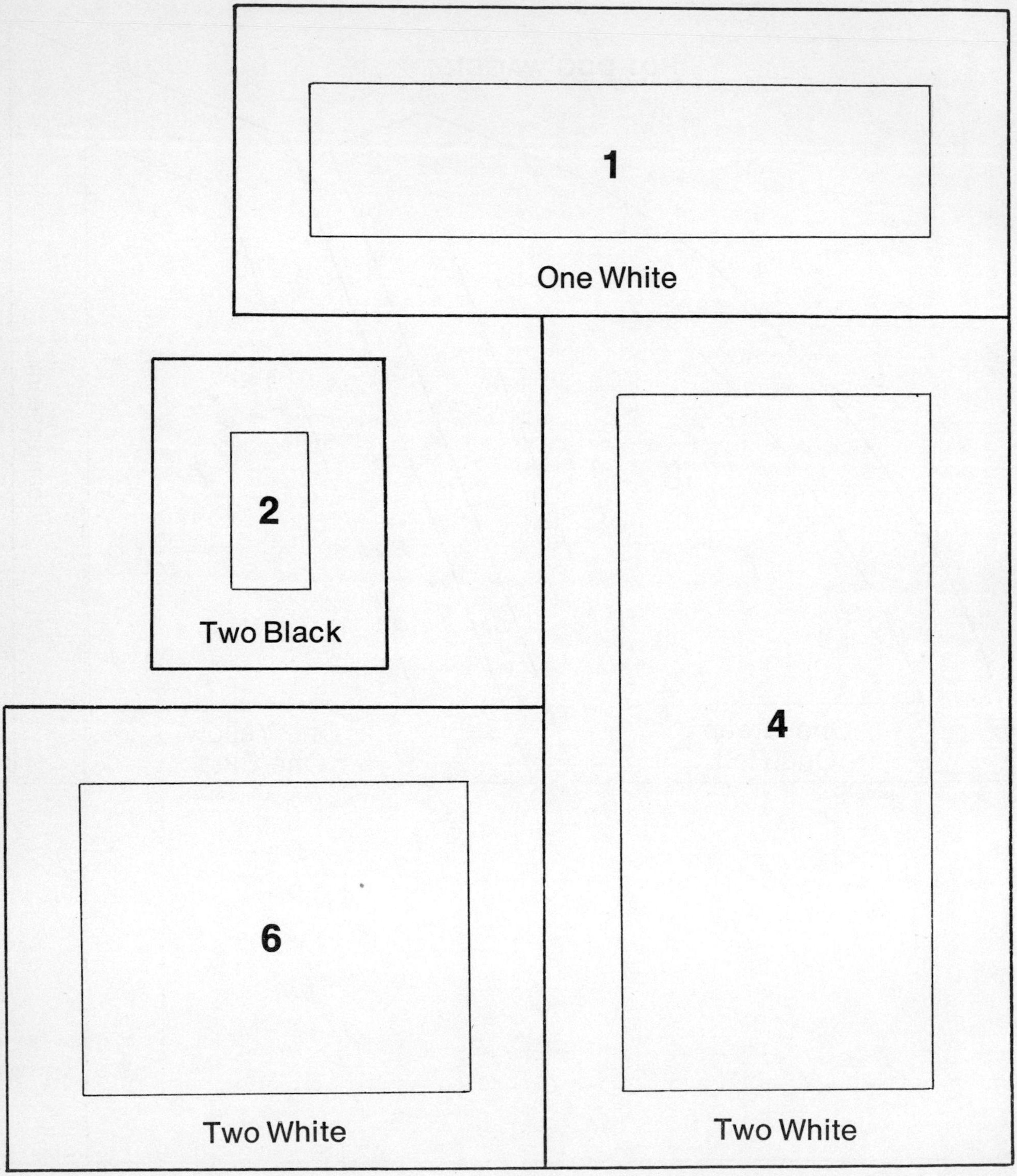

**1**

One White

**2**

Two Black

**4**

**6**

Two White

Two White

**HOT DOG WAGON**

5

One Orange

3

One Orange

**SHOP**

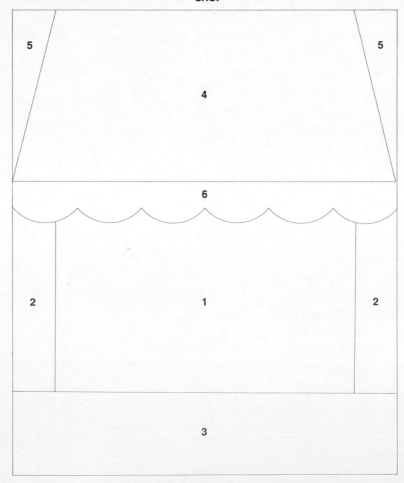

5     4     5

6

2     1     2

3

# SHOP

Suggested Colors: Green, Yellow, White

**Green:**

* Cut one of Pattern 4
* Cut one of Pattern 6 (plus facing)

**Yellow:**

Cut two of Pattern 2
* Cut one of Pattern 3
Cut two of Pattern 5

**White:**

Cut one of Pattern 1
* Patterns 3, 4, and 6 are cut on fold.

## STEP 1

Sew a 2 on each end of 1.

Sew 3 along the bottom of 1-2 (the side with no notches).

Sew a 5 on each side of 4, matching notches.

Lay 6 right side down on its facing and pin in place. Stitch a ¼-inch seam all around the scalloped edge, leaving the straight side open. Clip right to the stitching at the apex of each curve. Turn 6 right side out through the straight side and press the curves as neatly as possible. Press the other pieces completed in Step 1.

## STEP 2

Lay 6 right side up along its straight edge on 1-2, matching notches. Lay 4-5 right side down on 6, also matching notches.

Pin them all in place and sew. Press seam toward 4.

Optional: Embroider shop name on the awning.

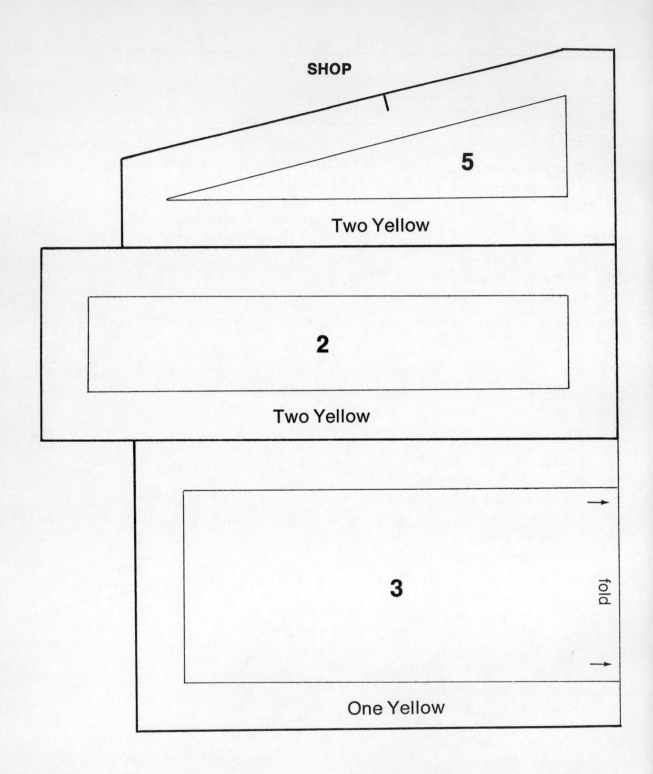

**SHOP**

**5**

Two Yellow

**2**

Two Yellow

**3**

fold

One Yellow

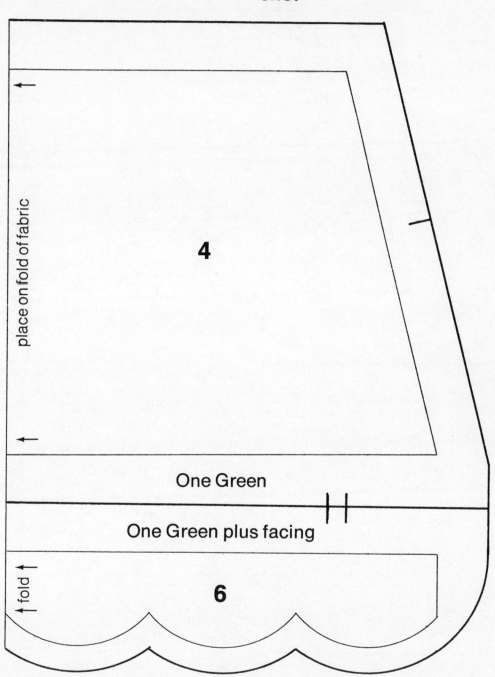

**SHOP**

4

place on fold of fabric

One Green

One Green plus facing

fold

6

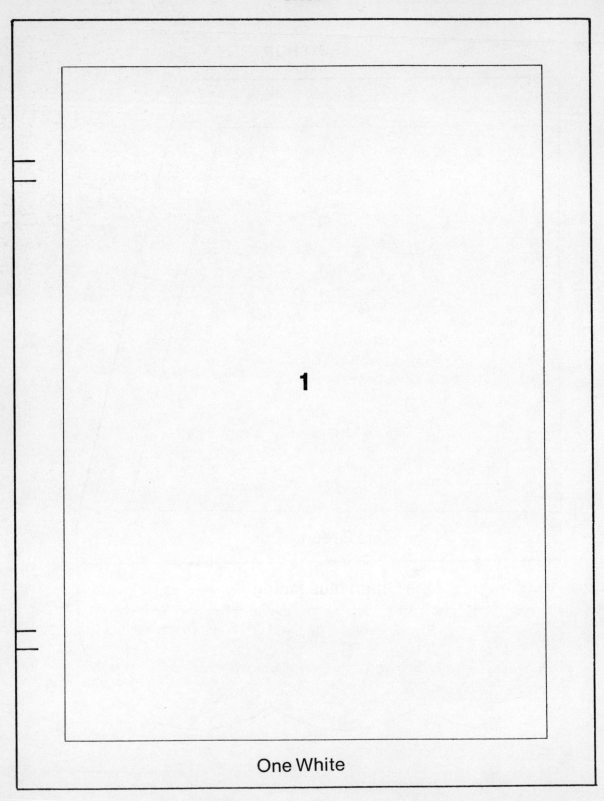

1

One White

**GOVERNMENT BUILDING**

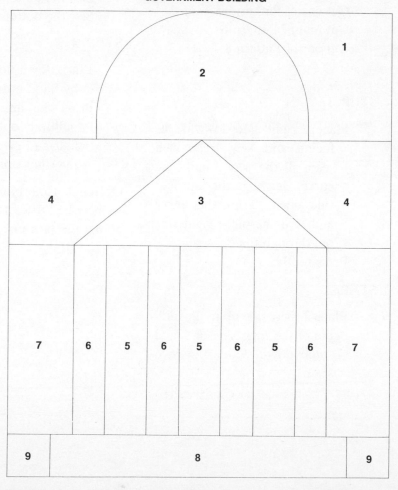

# GOVERNMENT BUILDING

Suggested Colors: White, Blue, Grey

**White:**

Cut one of Pattern 1

**Blue:**

Cut two of Pattern 4
Cut three of Pattern 5
Cut two of Pattern 7
Cut two of Pattern 9

**Grey:**

Cut one of Pattern 2 (plus facing)
Cut one of Pattern 3
Cut four of Pattern 6
Cut one of Pattern 8

## STEP 1

Place 2 right side down on its facing and sew a ½-inch seam all the way around the curve, leaving the straight side open. Trim the curve and turn the piece right side out through the open side.
Press neatly.

## STEP 2

Place 2 right side up in the middle of the long side of 1 and stitch down with a ¼-inch seam

Sew a 4 on each side of 3, matching notches.
Sew 5 and 6 pieces together alternately, with a 6 on each end.
Sew a 7 to each outside 6 piece.
Sew a 9 on each end of 8.
Press everything completed in Step 2.

## STEP 3

Sew 1-2 to 3-4.
Sew the bottom of 3-4 to 5-6-7.
Sew the bottom of 5-6-7 to 8-9.

## STEP 4

Pin 2 down flat on 1 and stitch by hand around curve.
Press the finished government building on the wrong side first and give a final press on the right side.

Optional: Embroider building name, such as FEDERAL HALL, on 8 or across the bottom of 3.

# GOVERNMENT BUILDING

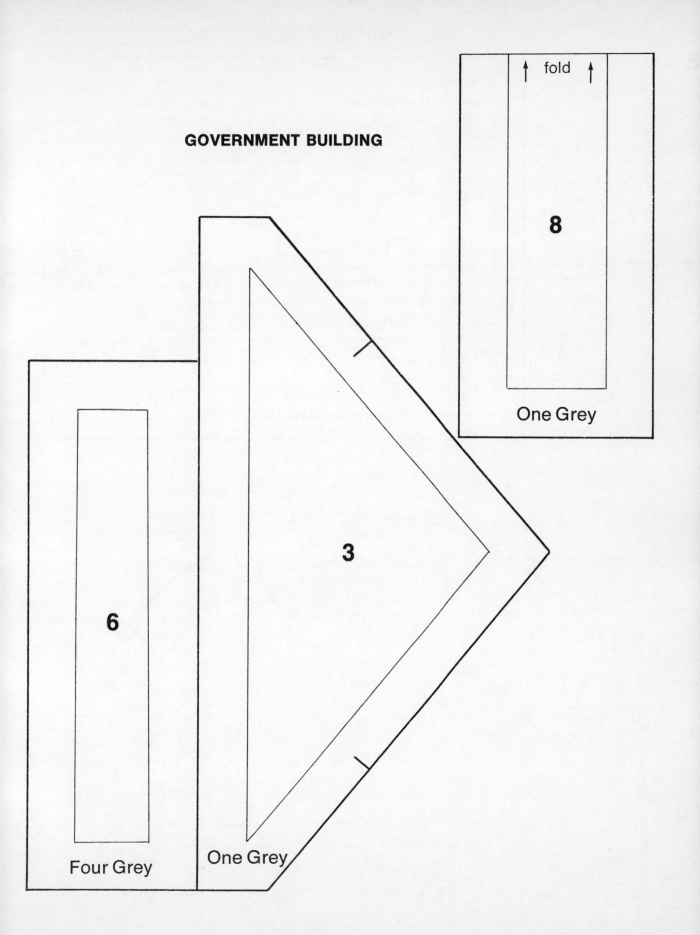

fold

8

One Grey

3

6

Four Grey

One Grey

# GOVERNMENT BUILDING

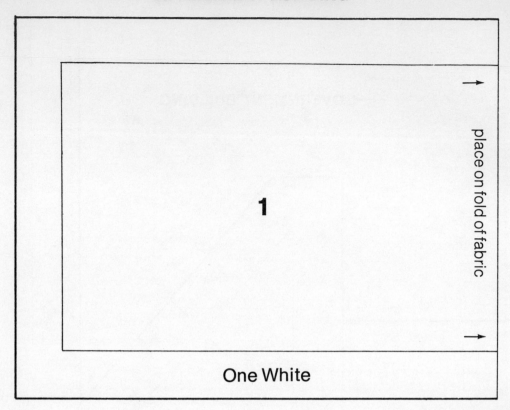

place on fold of fabric

**1**

One White

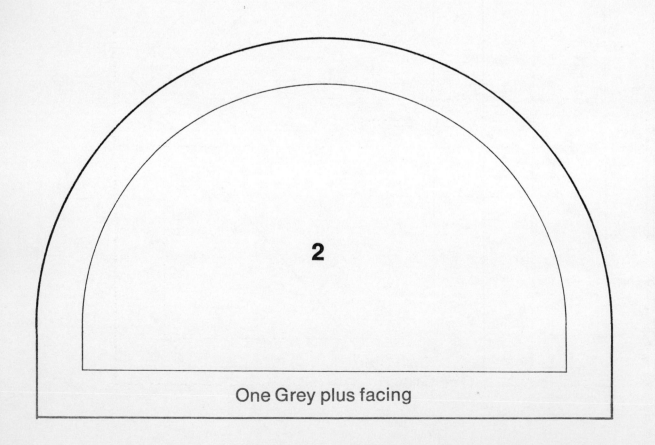

**2**

One Grey plus facing

# GOVERNMENT BUILDING

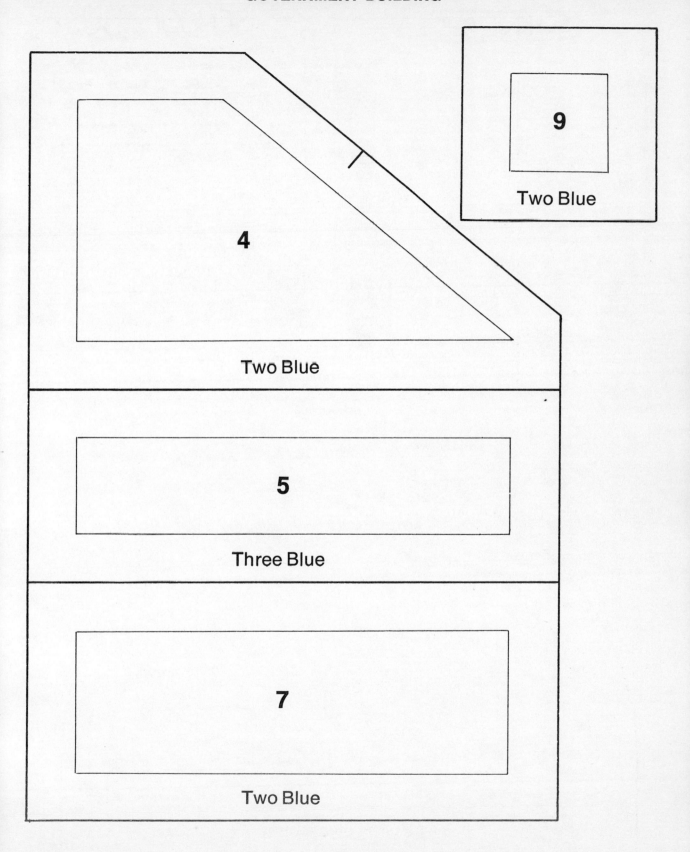

9

Two Blue

4

Two Blue

5

Three Blue

7

Two Blue

**SCHOOL BUS**

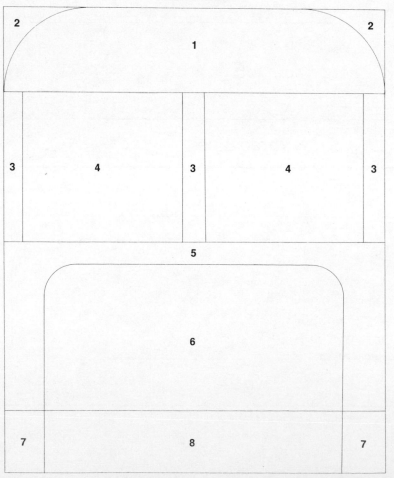

# SCHOOL BUS

Suggested Colors: Yellow, White, Black

**Yellow:**

Cut one of Pattern 1 (plus facing)
Cut three of Pattern 3
Cut one of Pattern 5
Cut one of Pattern 6 (plus facing)

**White:**

Cut one of Pattern 2
Cut two of Pattern 4
Cut one of Pattern 8

**Black:**

Cut two of Pattern 7

## STEP 1

Sew 1 and 6 face down on their matching facings with a ½-inch seam all the way around the curve, leaving the straight side open.

Trim the curve and turn right side out.

Sew the two 4 pieces and the three 3 pieces together in the alternating order as shown in diagram.

Sew a 7 on each end of 8.

Press everything at once taking care that the curves on 1 and 6 are done neatly.

## STEP 2

Sew the straight edge of 1 right side up along the long side of 2 with a ¼-inch seam.

Sew 3-4 to the bottom of 1-2.

Center 6 on the long side of 5 and stitch the pieces together with a ¼-inch seam.

Sew 7-8 to the bottom of 5-6.

Sew 1-2-3-4 to 5-6-7-8.

Press the entire block on the wrong side first with the seams away from 1-2 and 5-6.

## STEP 3

Pin the edges of 1 and 6 down and hem stitch by hand with small, invisible stitches.

Press on the right side.

Optional: Embroider SCHOOL BUS on 1 with a chain stitch and little red lights on each side of the sign. Embroider the large headlights in white.

**SCHOOL BUS**

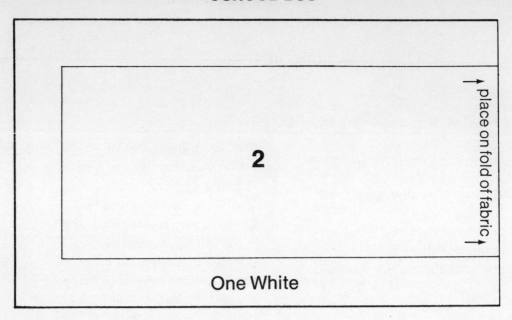

**2**

place on fold of fabric

One White

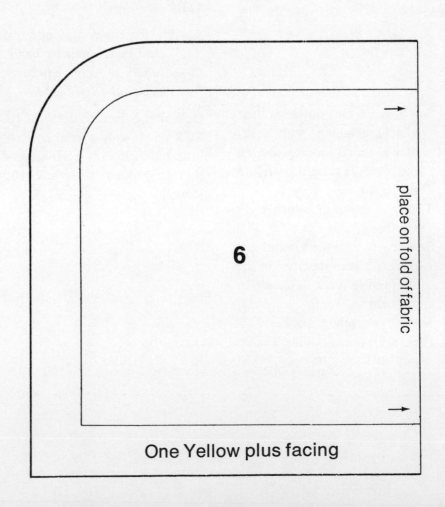

**6**

place on fold of fabric

One Yellow plus facing

# SCHOOL BUS

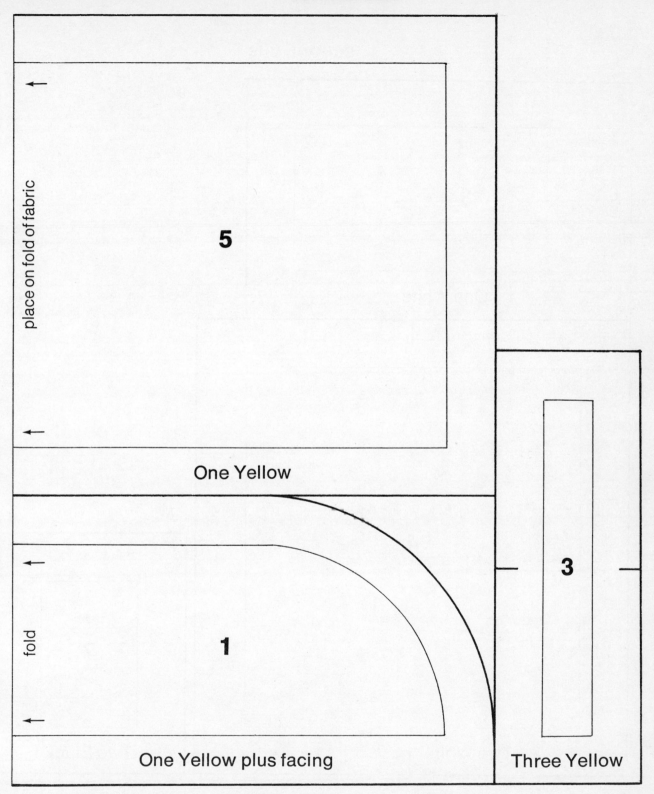

place on fold of fabric

**5**

One Yellow

fold

**1**

One Yellow plus facing

**3**

Three Yellow

# SCHOOL BUS

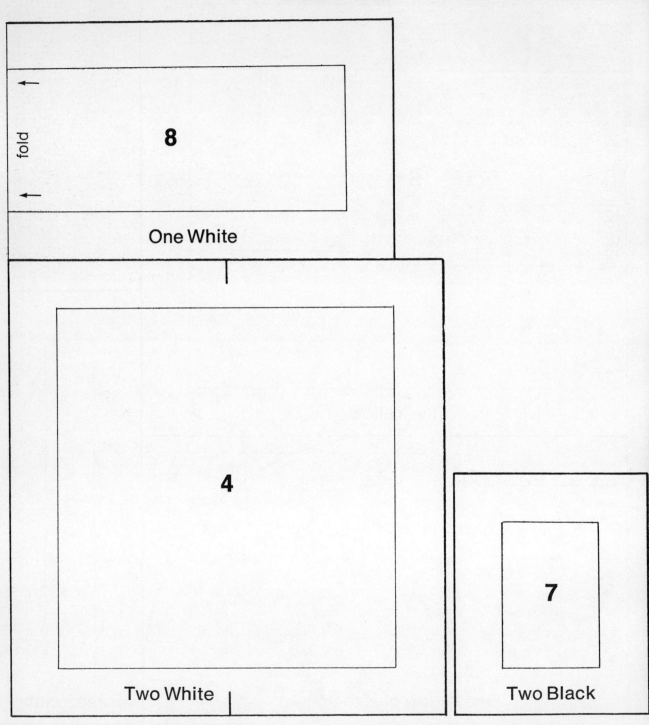

**8**

fold

One White

**4**

Two White

**7**

Two Black

**ARMORY**

| | | |
|---|---|---|
| 3 | 4 | 1 1 1 1 1 1 2 |
| | | 10 |
| 1 1 1 1 2 | | 7 8 9 |
| 3 | | |
| | | 9 8 7 |
| 5 | | 7 8 9 |
| 6 | | 9 8 7 |
| | | 10 |

# ARMORY or CASTLE

Suggested Colors: Grey, Black, White

**Grey:**

Cut one of Pattern 1
Cut one of Pattern 2
Cut one of Pattern 3
* Cut one of Pattern 5 (plus facing)
Cut two of Pattern 7
Cut two of Pattern 9
Cut two of Pattern 10

**Black:**

* Cut one of Pattern 6
Cut two of Pattern 8

**White:**

Cut one of Pattern 1
Cut one of Pattern 3
Cut one of Pattern 4

* 5 and 6 are cut on the fold of the fabric

## STEP 1

Sew the grey 1 and the white 1 together lengthwise to make one strip.
Press the seam toward the grey side.
Measure this strip into five 1½-inch pieces. Mark and cut.

Sew three of these blocks together side by side, alternating colors.
Sew the remaining two together side by side.
Cut 2 in half and sew one half to the white end of each row completed above. You now have a row of five and a row of seven blocks.
Press seams in one direction.

## STEP 2

Sew the grey 3 on the bottom of the row of five blocks completed above.
Sew the white 3 on top of the row of five blocks.
Sew a 10 to the bottom of the row of seven blocks.
Press everything.

## STEP 3

Sew 4 to the right of the tower (1-2-3).
Place 5 right side down on top of its facing, pin in place and stitch ½ inch all the way around the curve. Trim the seam, turn the piece right side out, and press neatly. Treat 5 and its facing as one piece.
Place 5 on top of 6 and pin together. Hand sew the curve of 5 to 6 with tiny stitches.

*114*

## STEP 4

Sew 7, 8, and 9 together side by side. Repeat.

Press the seams in one direction. Fold both sections of 7-8-9 neatly in half and press the fold into a crease. Cut along this crease (the dotted line indicated on the pattern pieces 7, 8, and 9).

Look at the diagram and arrange these four window sections in the order indicated.

Sew together.

Sew the 1-2-10 piece completed in Step 1 on the top of the windows and the remaining 10 to the bottom.

Press.

## STEP 5

Sew 5-6 to the bottom of 1-2-3-4.

Sew 7-8-9-10 to the right side of this piece.

Press on both sides.

**ARMORY**

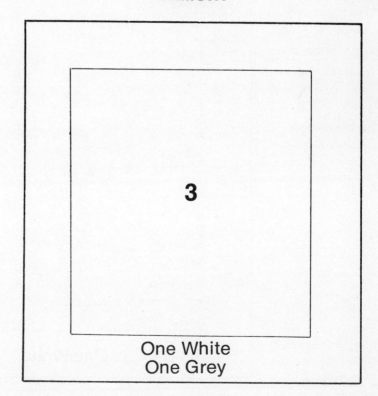

3

One White
One Grey

# ARMORY

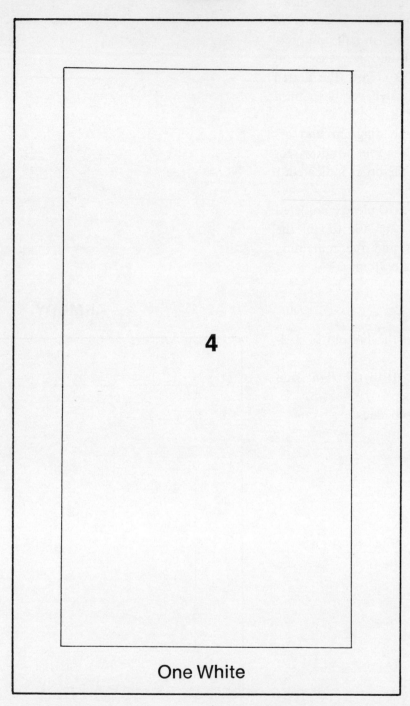

**4**

One White

**ARMORY**

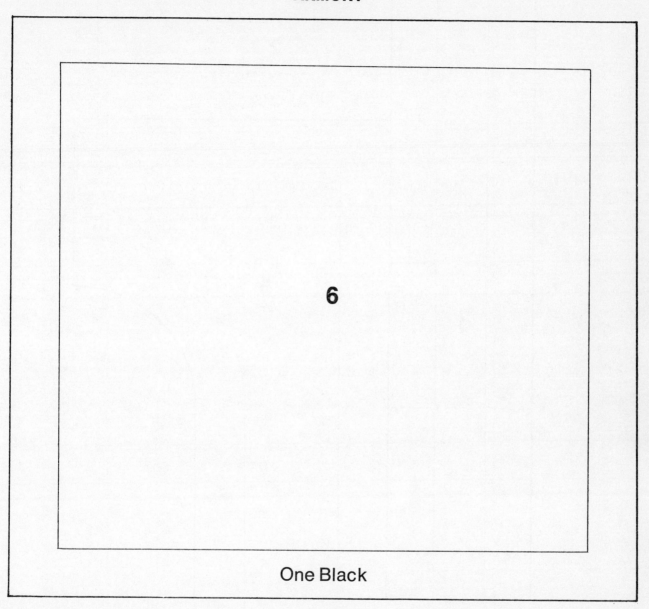

6

One Black

# ARMORY

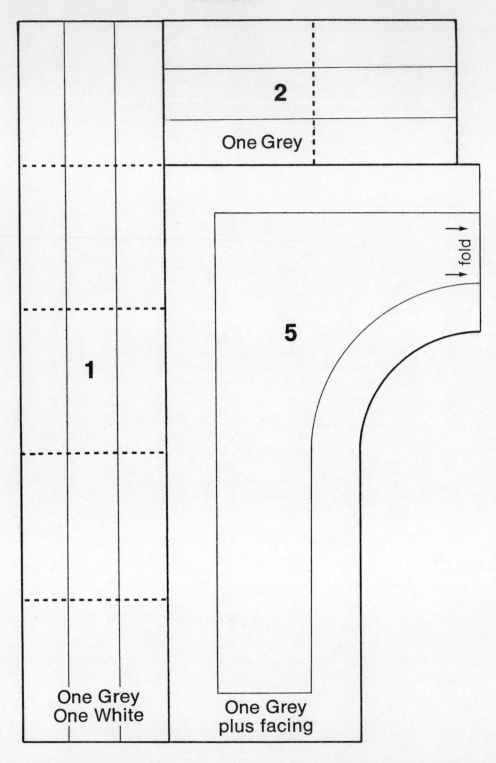

**2**

One Grey

**1**

One Grey
One White

**5**

fold

One Grey
plus facing

# ARMORY

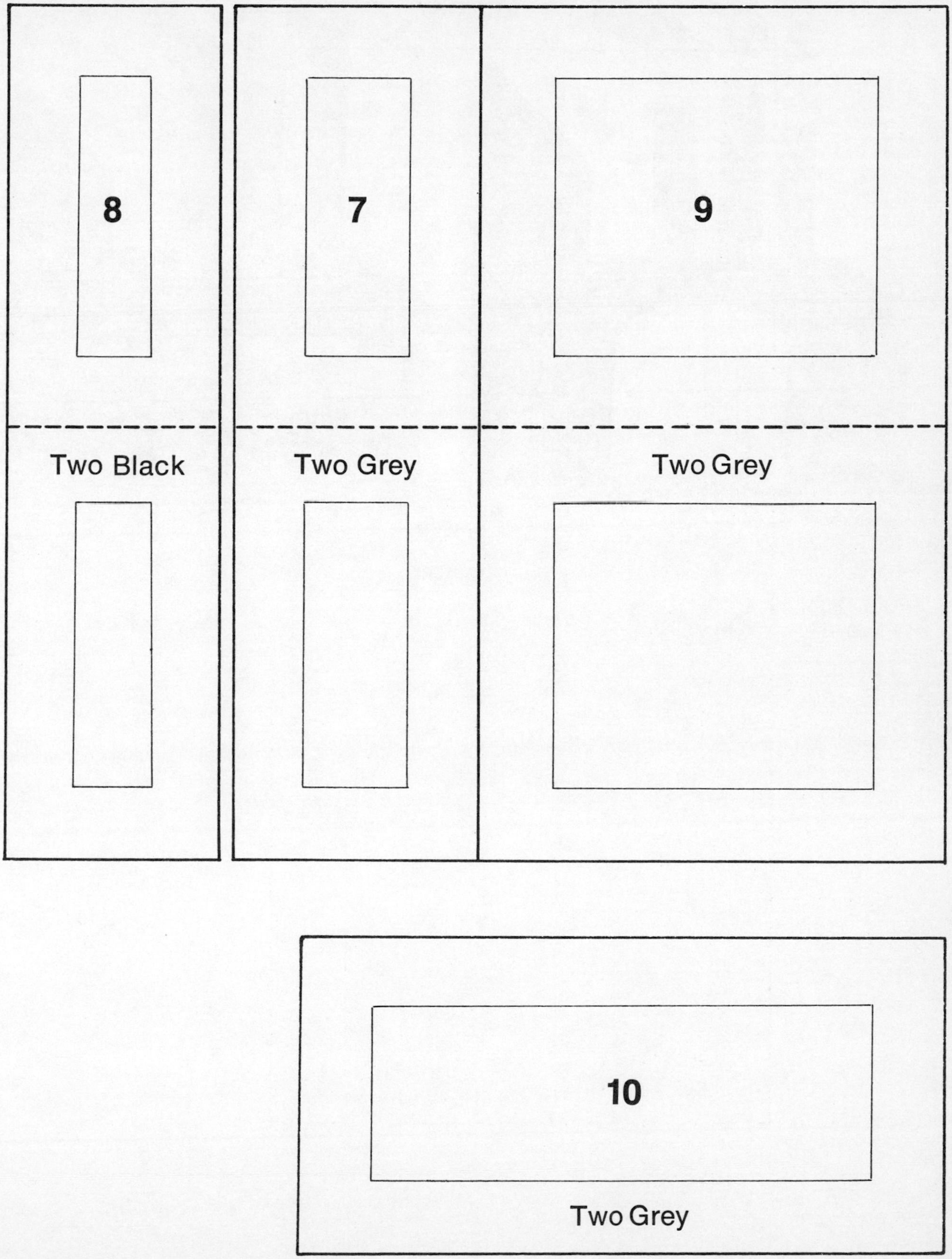

**8**

**7**

**9**

Two Black

Two Grey

Two Grey

**10**

Two Grey

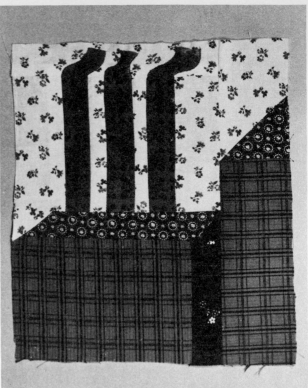

**FACTORY**

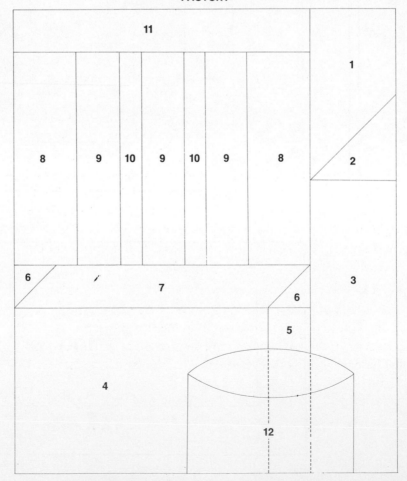

# FACTORY

Suggested Colors: White, Purple, Blue, Black

**White:**

Cut one of Pattern 1
Cut one of Pattern 6
Cut two of Pattern 8
Cut two of Pattern 10
Cut one of Pattern 11
Cut one of Pattern 12 (plus facing)

**Purple:**

Cut one of Pattern 2
Cut one of Pattern 7

**Blue:**

Cut one of Pattern 3
Cut one of Pattern 4
Cut three of Pattern 9

**Black:**

Cut one of Pattern 5
Cut one of Pattern 6

## STEP 1

Sew 1 and 2 together, matching notches.
Sew 3 to 2.
Sew 5 to the right of 4.
Sew a 6 to either end of 7, matching notches—the white on the left, the black on the right.
Sew all the 8, 9, and 10 pieces together in the order indicated by the diagram.
Sew 12 right side down on its facing with a ½-inch seam, leaving the straight side open. Trim curve. Turn right side out and press.
While at the ironing board press all pieces completed in Step 1.

## STEP 2

Sew 4-5 to 6-7.
Sew 8-9-10 to the top of 6-7.
Sew 11 to the top of 8-9-10.
Press everything.

## STEP 3

Sew 1-2-3 down the right side of the piece completed in Step 2.
Pin the oil tank (12) to the factory, matching the straight edge to the bottom of the block. Hand sew with small invisible hem stitches all the way around the tank. Press first on wrong side and give the block a final press on the right side.

Optional: Embroider a ladder up the side of the tank and smoke coming out of the smokestacks. The oil tank can be left out altogether if desired.

To top the smokestacks in red and white stripes sew a piece of striped fabric to a piece of blue before cutting out Pattern 9.

*121*

**FACTORY**

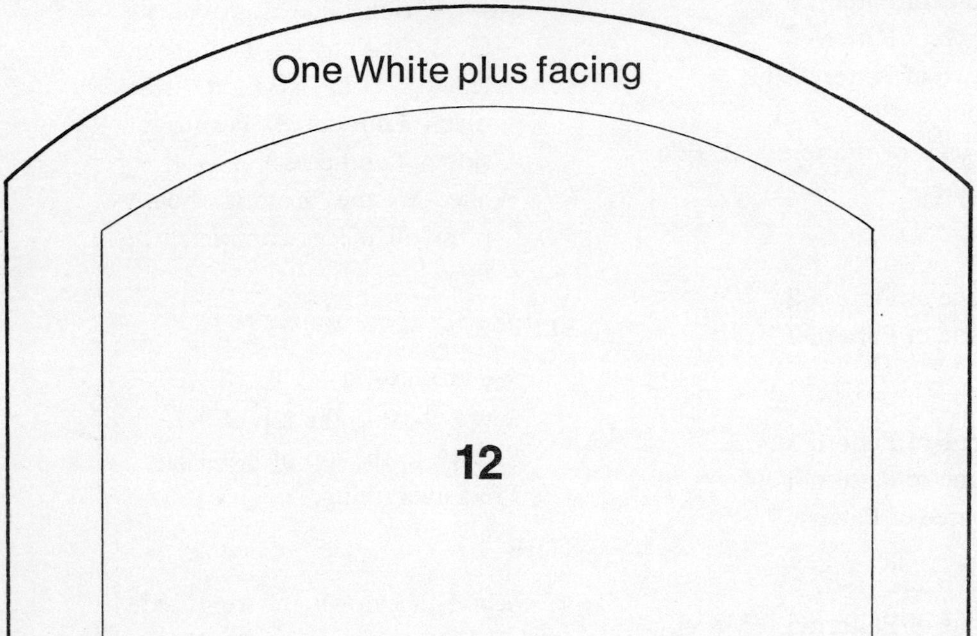

One White plus facing

**12**

**FACTORY**

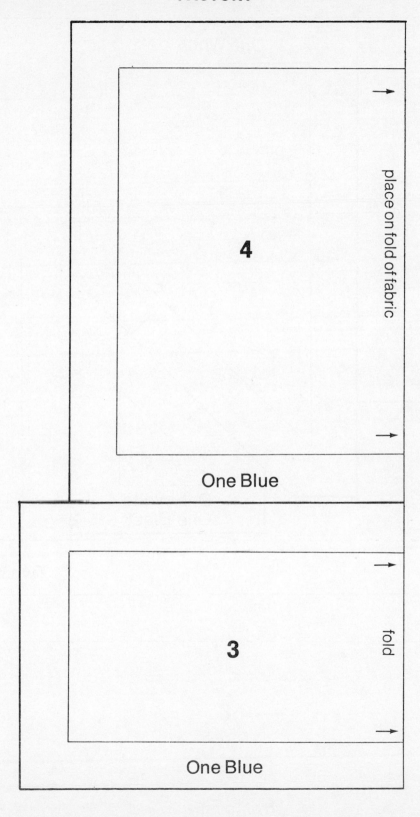

4

place on fold of fabric

One Blue

3

fold

One Blue

# FACTORY

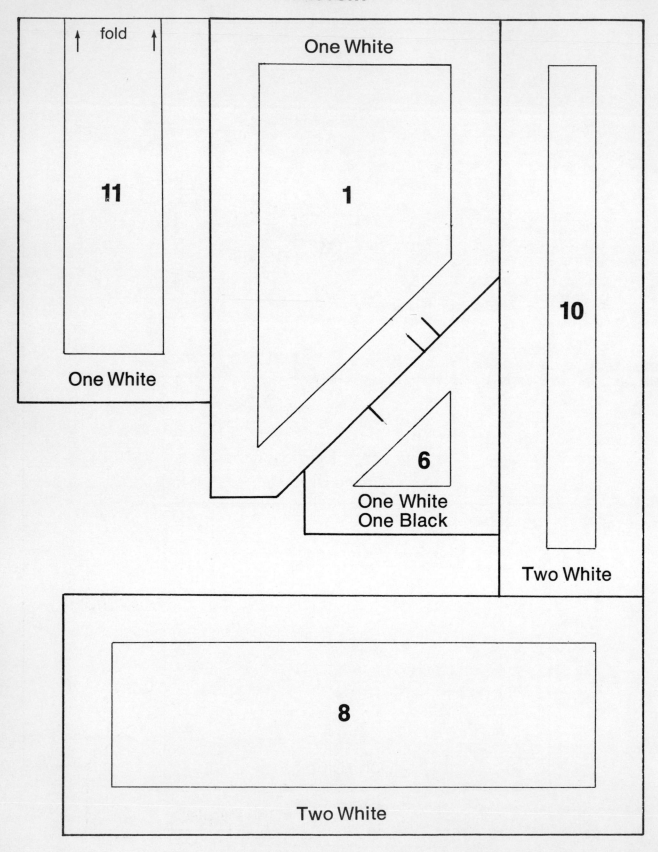

fold

One White

**11**

One White

One White

**1**

**10**

**6**

One White
One Black

Two White

**8**

Two White

**FACTORY**

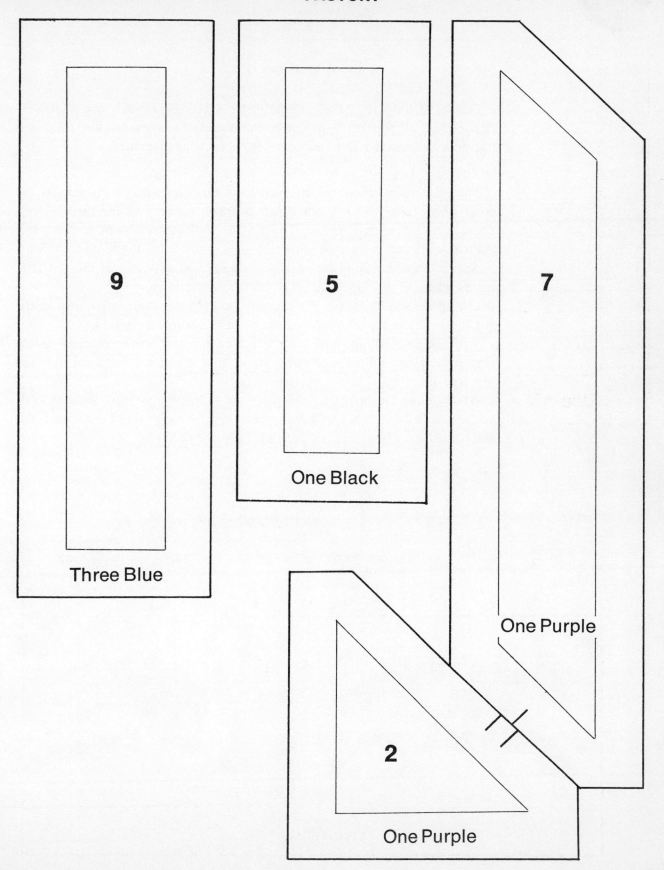

9

5

7

Three Blue

One Black

One Purple

2

One Purple

The CHURCH, STREET SWEEPER, BROWNSTONE, and MOVIE HOUSE are all patterns that require the turning of a corner. The following instructions describe how to turn corners on a sewing machine.

### DOTS

There are always three pattern pieces involved in turning a corner. At the point where they meet is a dot which is drawn on each of the three pieces. These dots mark the pivot point. The notches mark where 2 joins 3.

First sew 1 and 2 together with a ½-inch seam. Press the seam up toward 1. Sew 3 down the side of 1 with a ½-inch seam and stop at the dot (the corner where all three pieces meet) with the needle down.

Lift up the sewing foot of the machine and clip the seam allowance to the dot. This releases the fabric so you can pivot and adjust the pieces.

With the foot still up, turn 3 and place on top of 2 so the notches match, stretch the fabric a little, and check to see that 2 is flat. Lower the foot and sew 2 to 3.

When you're finished, take the piece out, turn it over, and look at it. If you're satisfied that it is neatly done press on the wrong side so the seam is flat and turned away from 3. Then press again on the right side.

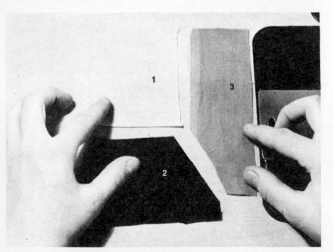
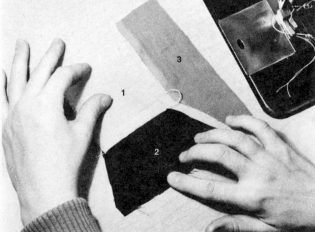

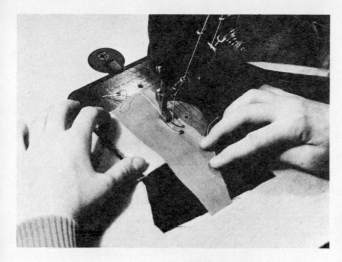 

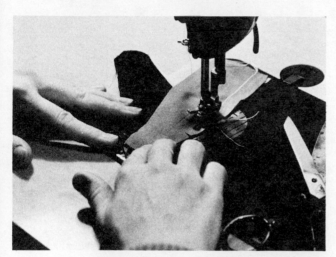 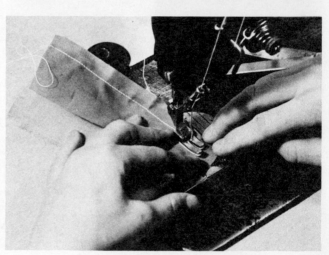

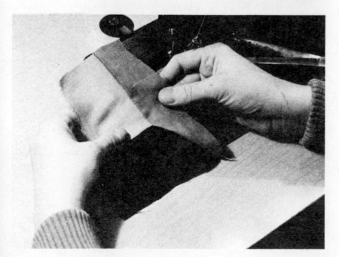

*To turn a neat corner at the intersection of three pieces: Sew 1 and 2 together as shown, then sew 3 down the side of 1 and 2 to dot indicated on pattern. Lift the machine foot and clip to dot. With the foot still up, adjust the fabric so that the notches on 2 and 3 match. Sew 3 to 2 as shown.*

CHURCH

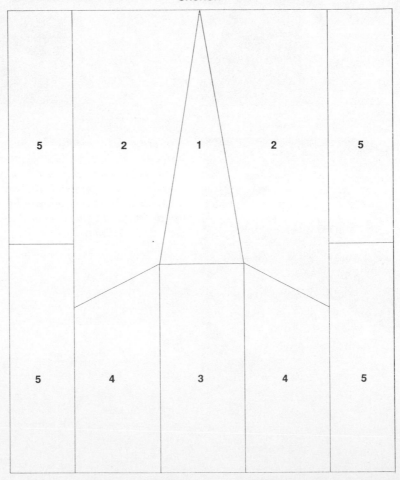

## CHURCH

Suggested Colors: Grey, White

**Grey:**

Cut one of Pattern 1
Cut one of Pattern 3
Cut two of Pattern 4
Cut two of Pattern 5

**White:**

Cut two of Pattern 2
Cut two of Pattern 5

STEP 1

Sew a 2 down each side of 1, matching notches.
Sew a 4 down each side of 3.
Sew a grey 5 to each white 5 end to end.
Press everything.

STEP 2

Sew 2-1-2 to 4-3-4 by joining 2 and 4 at the ends and matching notches. Stop with the needle down at the dot.
Lift up the foot, clip to the dot, adjust the fabric (1 and 3) until smooth and stitch. Repeat at next dot, neatly joining 2 to 4.

STEP 3

Sew the 5 pieces (grey end on the bottom) to both sides of the church.
Press on wrong side first. Turn and press again on right side.

# CHURCH

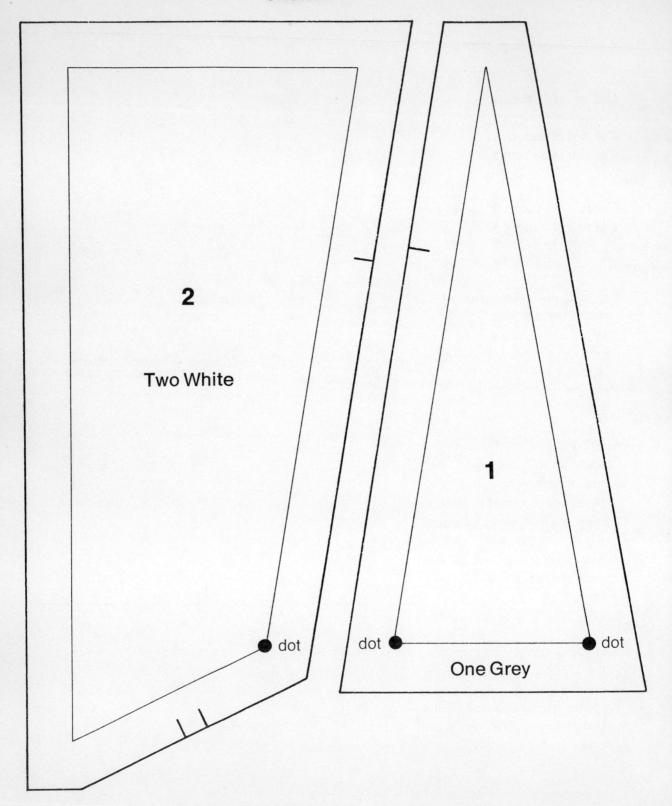

**2**

Two White

**1**

dot

dot    One Grey    dot

CHURCH

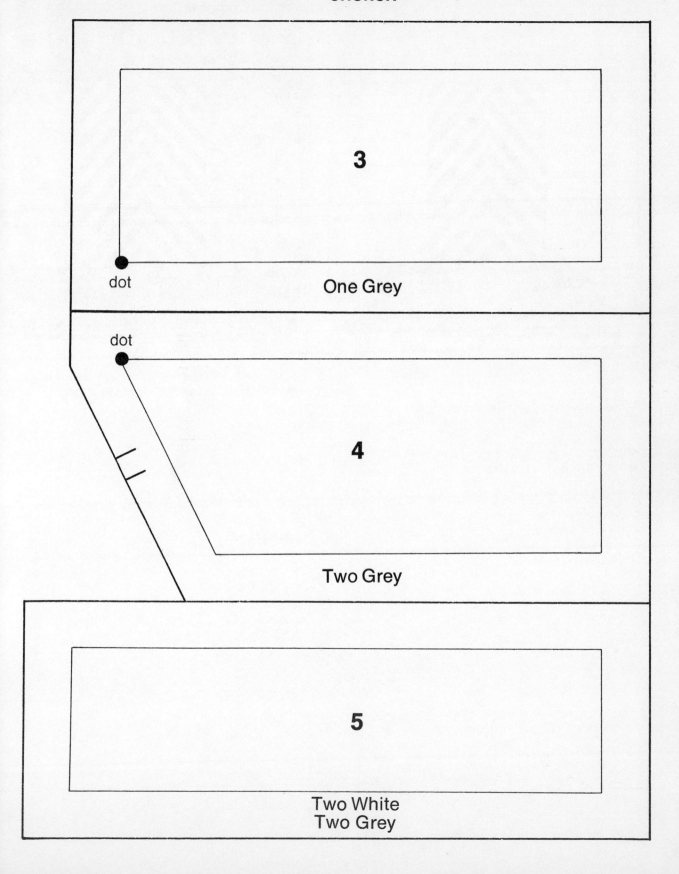

**3**

dot

One Grey

dot

**4**

Two Grey

**5**

Two White
Two Grey

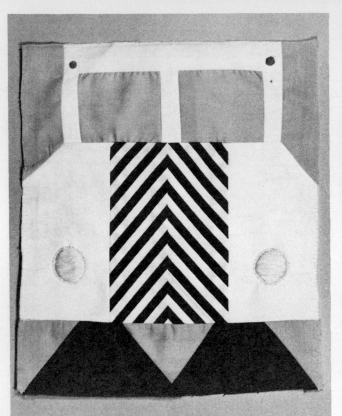

## STREET SWEEPER

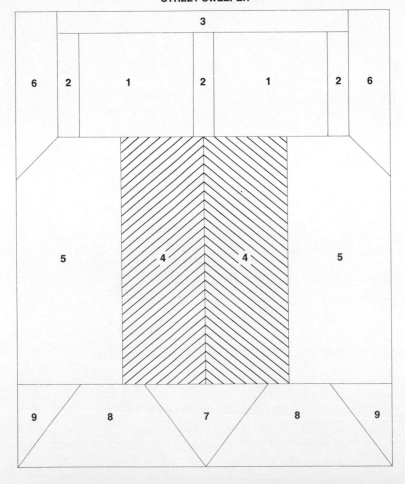

# STREET SWEEPER

Suggested Colors: Stripe, Light Grey, White, Brown

**Stripe:**

   * Cut two of Pattern 4 (bias)

**Light Grey:**

   Cut two of Pattern 1
   ** Cut two of Pattern 6

Cut one of Pattern 7
** Cut two of Pattern 9

**White:**

Cut three of Pattern 2
Cut one of Pattern 3
Cut two of Pattern 5

**Brown:**

** Cut two of Pattern 8

* For 4, place the pattern on a piece of fabric that is folded in half. Be sure the direction of the stripe in the pattern matches the direction of the stripe in the fabric (bias). Don't forget to clip the notch. These two pieces will be sewn together down the side marked with the notch.

* For pieces 6, 8, and 9 the fabric should be folded. This insures that the duplicate of each piece will be in the reverse and when all pieces are assembled there will be no trouble with the fit.

STEP 1

   To make the windows, sew all the 1 and 2 pieces together in the order indicated in the diagram.

   Sew both 4 pieces together down the center matching stripes.

   This makes the grill. Sew both 5 pieces down either side of 4.

   Sew the 7, 8, and 9 pieces together in the order indicated in the diagram, matching notches. These are the brushes.

   Press everything.

STEP 2

   Sew 3 on top of 1 and 2 (windows). Press seam toward 3.

STEP 3

   Sew 4 and 5 to the bottom of 1, 2, and 3.

   Sew 6 down each side of the windows to the dot, lift up foot, clip to dot, pivot, adjust 5 and 6 so the notches match, stretch a little, and sew.

   Sew 7, 8, and 9 to the bottom of 4 and 5.

   Press the finished piece on the wrong side first and then on the right side.

Optional: Embroider little red lights on each end of 3 and big yellow headlights in the middle of each 5.

*133*

**STREET SWEEPER**

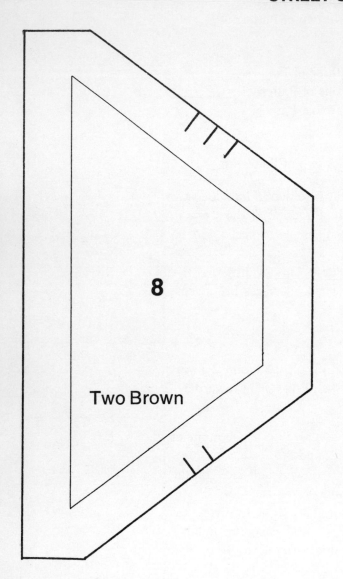

**8**

Two Brown

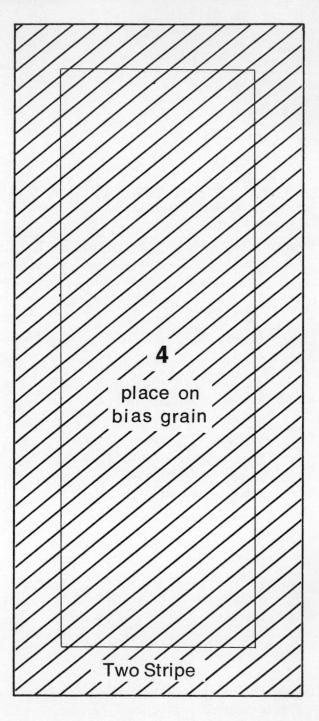

**4**

place on
bias grain

Two Stripe

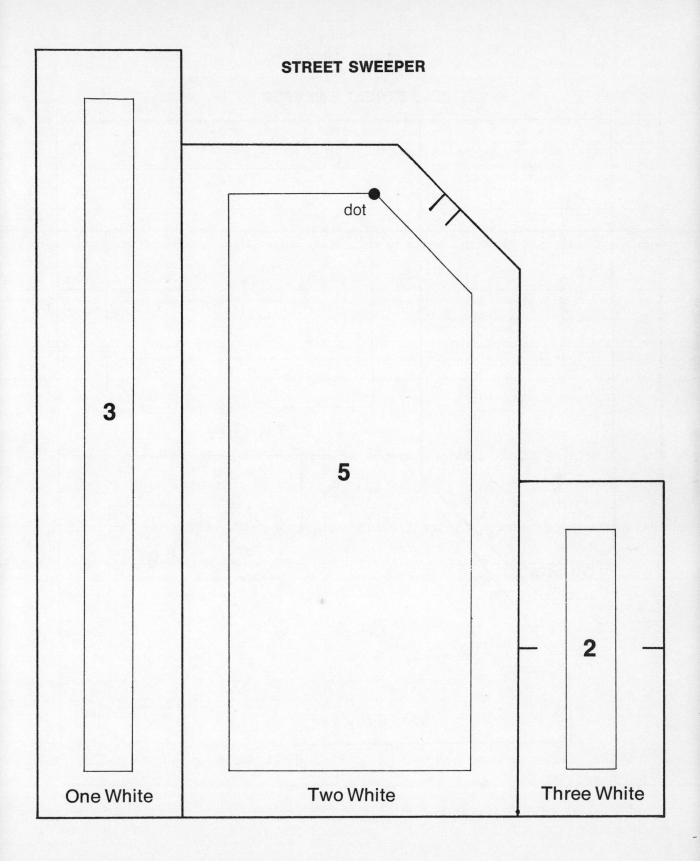

STREET SWEEPER

dot

3

5

2

One White                    Two White                    Three White

# STREET SWEEPER

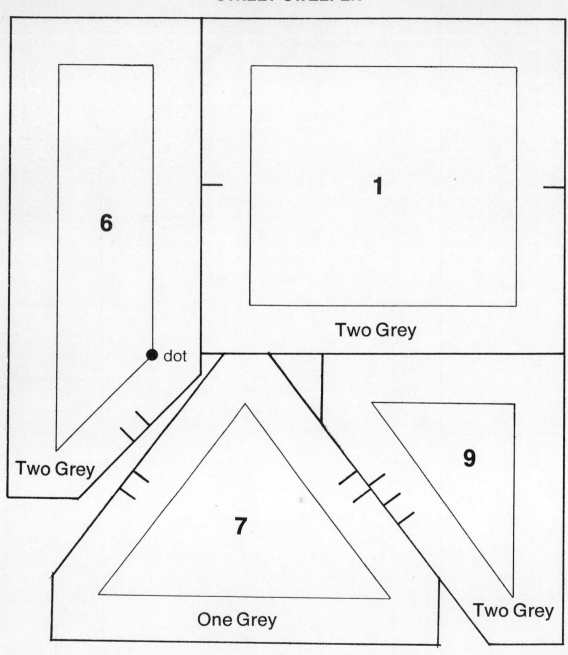

## BROWNSTONE

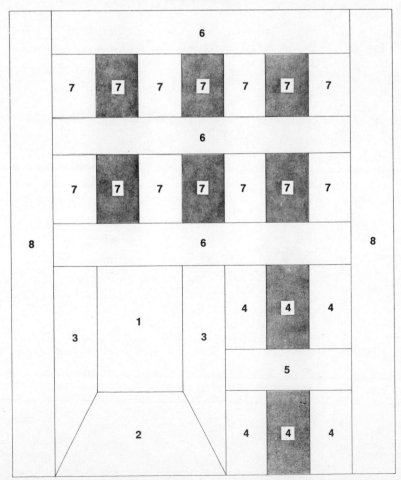

## BROWNSTONE

Suggested Colors: Green, Black, Brown, White

**Green:**

Cut one of Pattern 1

**Black:**

Cut one of Pattern 2

**Brown:**

Cut two of Pattern 3
Cut two of Pattern 4
Cut one of Pattern 5
Cut three of Pattern 6
Cut four of Pattern 7

**White:**

Cut one of Pattern 4
Cut three of Pattern 7
Cut two of Pattern 8

STEP 1

Sew 1 to 2 as in diagram.
Sew a 3 down each side of 1 to the dot, stop with the needle down, lift up the foot, clip to the dot, pivot, adjust the fabric so the notches on 2 and 3 match smoothly, stretch a little, and sew 3 to 2.
Press seams away from 3.

STEP 2

Sew a brown 4 down each side of the white 4.

Sew the brown and white 7 pieces together lengthwise, alternating the colors so you have a brown one on each end.

Press both sections with the seams going in one direction.

Fold each section neatly in half and press the fold into a crease. Cut both sections in half along this crease (which is indicated on the pattern pieces 4 and 7 by a broken line).

You now have four rows of windows.

STEP 3

Sew 5 between the two rows of 4.

Sew the two rows of 7 between the three 6 pieces lengthwise.

Press both sections with the seams in one direction.

STEP 4

Sew 4-5 along the right side of 1-2-3.

Sew that section on the bottom of 6-7.

Sew an 8 down the full length of each side of the brownstone.

Optional: Embroider a street address on the door and flower boxes in the windows and, perhaps, a banister down the steps to the sidewalk.

**BROWNSTONE**

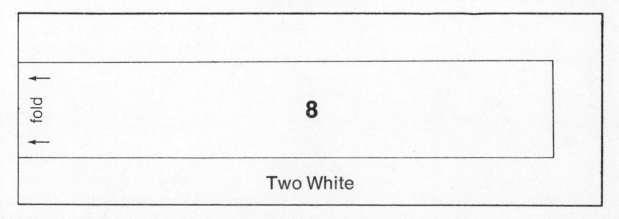

139

# BROWNSTONE

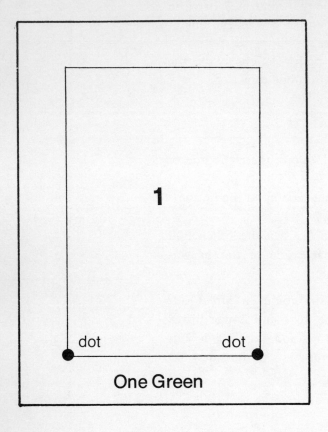

1

dot          dot

One Green

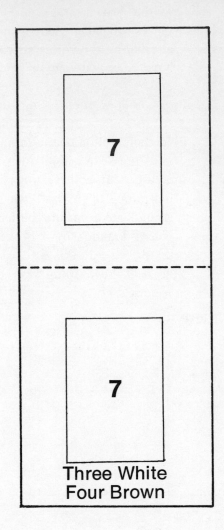

7

7

Three White
Four Brown

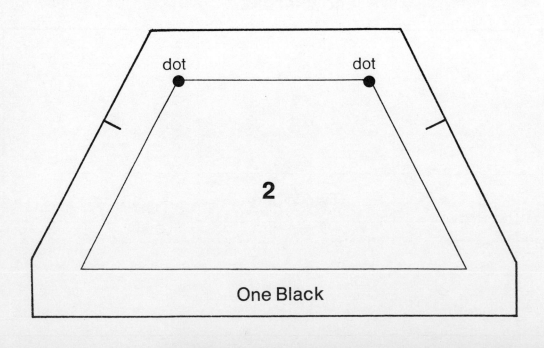

dot          dot

2

One Black

# BROWNSTONE

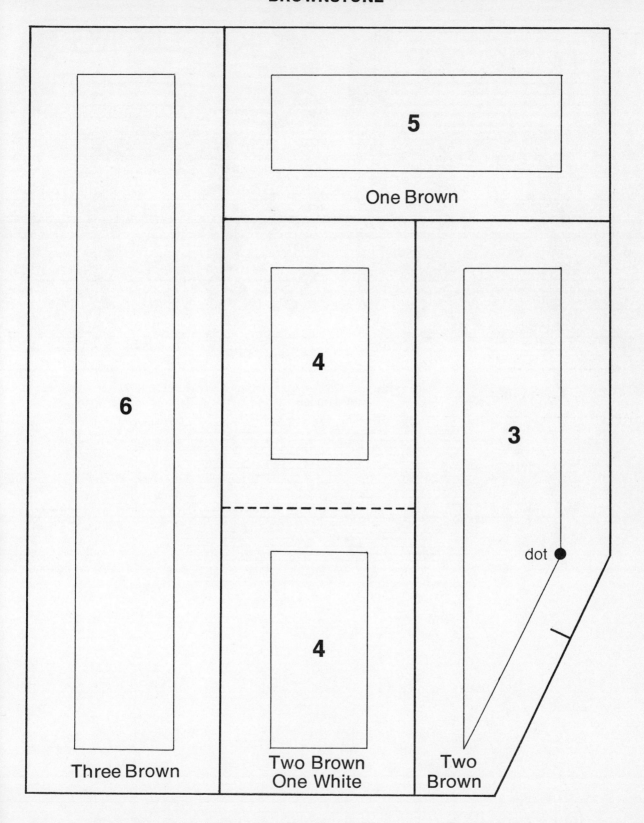

**5**

One Brown

**6**

**4**

**3**

dot

**4**

Three Brown

Two Brown
One White

Two
Brown

**MOVIE HOUSE**

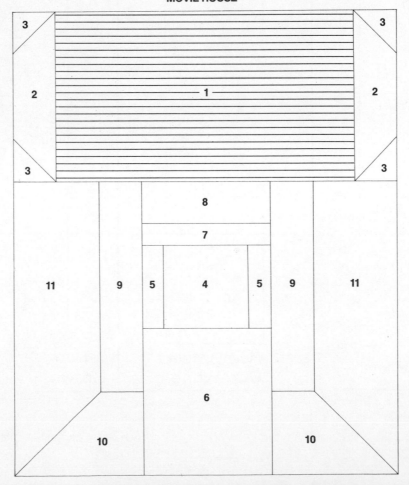

# MOVIE HOUSE

Suggested Colors: Stripe, Blue, Red, White

**Stripe:**

Cut one of Pattern 1

**Blue:**

Cut two of Pattern 2
Cut one of Pattern 8
Cut two of Pattern 9
Cut two of Pattern 10

**Red:**

Cut four of Pattern 3
Cut two of Pattern 5
Cut one of Pattern 6
Cut one of Pattern 7
Cut two of Pattern 11

**White:**

Cut one of Pattern 4

STEP 1

Sew a 2 on each end of 1.
Sew a 3 to each corner of 2, matching notches.
Sew a 5 to opposite sides of 4.
Sew 6 to the bottom of 4-5.
Sew 7 along the top of 4-5.
Sew 8 to the top of 7.
Sew the short end of 10 to the short end of 9. Repeat.
Press everything.

STEP 2

Sew 4-5-6-7-8 between the two pieces of 9-10, checking the diagram for the proper layout.
Sew 11 down the side of 9 to the dot, stop with the needle down, lift up the foot, clip to the dot, adjust the fabric so 10 and 11 match at the notches, stretch a little, and sew. Repeat.
Press neatly on both sides.

STEP 3

Sew the top section 1-2-3 to the bottom section completed in Step 2.
Press.

Optional: Embroider the title of your favorite movie on the marquee (1).

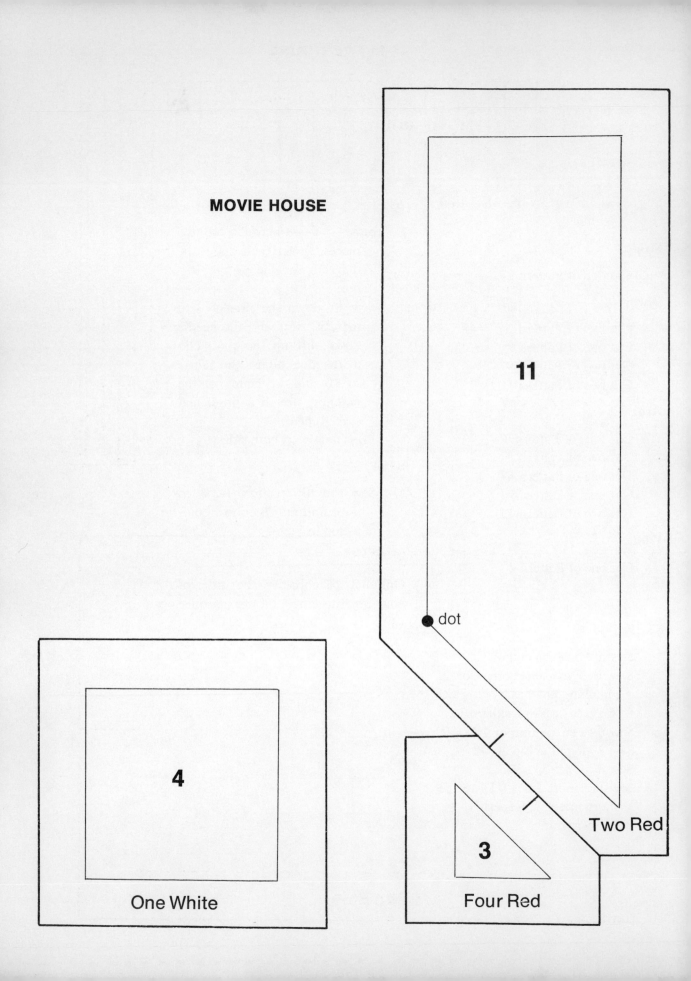

MOVIE HOUSE

**11**

dot

Two Red

**4**

One White

**3**

Four Red

# MOVIE HOUSE

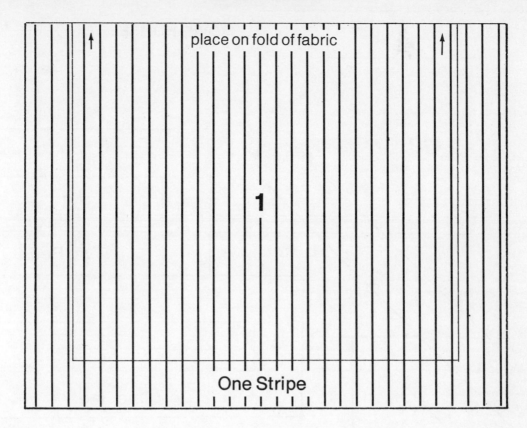

place on fold of fabric

**1**

One Stripe

**8**

One Blue

**9**

Two Blue

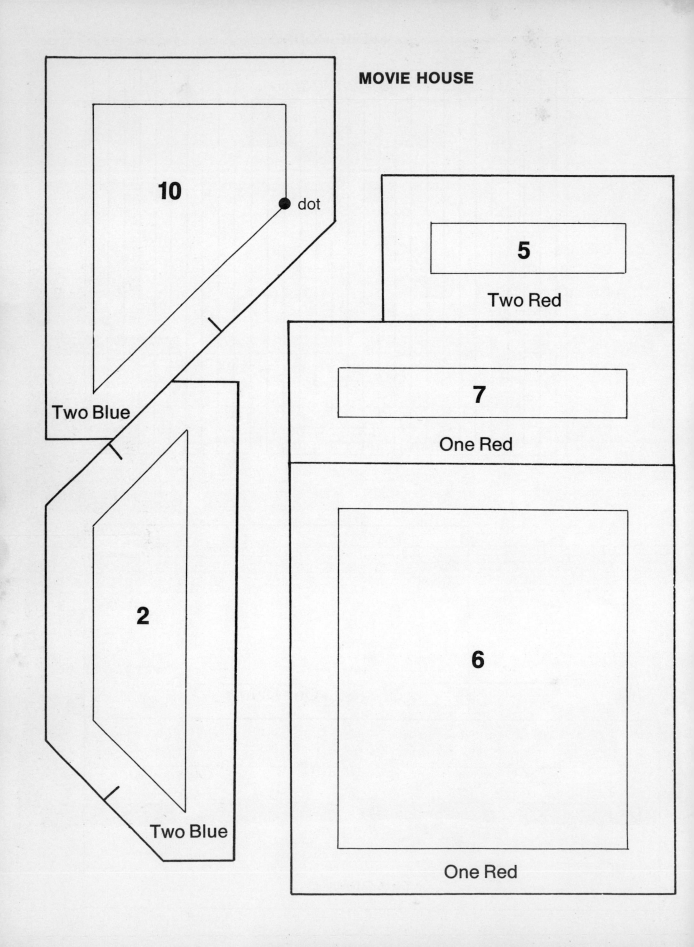

**MOVIE HOUSE**

10

dot

Two Blue

5

Two Red

7

One Red

2

Two Blue

6

One Red

*The Bradshaw Quilt*

*The Belinda Quilt*

*The Stuart Quilt*

*Annie's Quilt made for Anne Nitschke, of Silks, Satins, and Velvets*

## SET-IN CURVES

A "set-in" curve is not difficult as long as the pieces you're working with aren't too small. When cutting out the pieces be sure to clip each notch right to the stitching line. These deep notches are necessary for this kind of curve only, and they are the only ones drawn this way.

First machine stitch around the curve of 1-2-1 on the sewing line indicated on the pattern pieces. This line is ½ inch from the cutting line. Stitch around the curve of 3 on the sewing line.

Next, set 3 into 1-2-1 by matching the notches (right sides in) and pinning at each notch. Stretch a little if necessary while pinning so the notches match and the stitching lines are on top of each other. Before sewing turn the pieces right side up and make sure the bottom edges are even. Re-pin if necessary.

When you are ready, machine stitch without basting around the entire curve, easing and adjusting as you go. Otherwise, baste first. To make a smooth curve ease 3 into 1-2-1 slowly and carefully, being sure to sew on top of the stitching line.

Press on the wrong side with the seam turned away from 1. Then give the piece a final press on the right side.

*To sew a set-in curve: Stitch around both curves and pin the two pieces together as shown. Sew the pieces together, stitching on top of the first stitching. Ease and readjust fabric as you stitch so that the fit is smooth.*

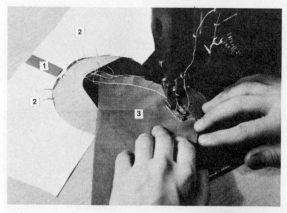

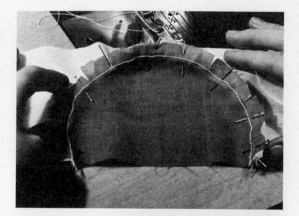

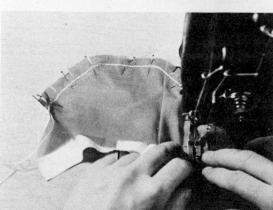

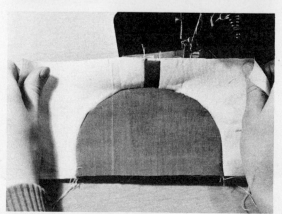

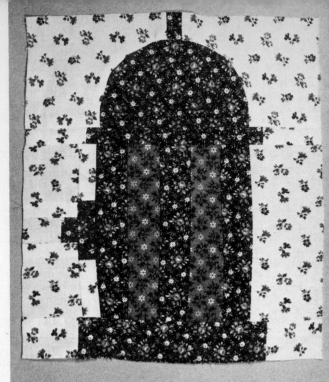

FIRE HYDRANT

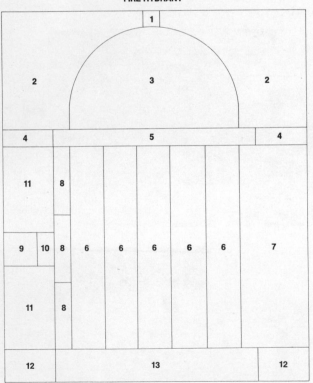

## FIRE HYDRANT

Suggested Colors: Black, Red, White

**Black:**

Cut one of Pattern 1
Cut one of Pattern 3
Cut one of Pattern 5
Cut three of Pattern 6
Cut one of Pattern 8
Cut one of Pattern 10
Cut one of Pattern 13

**Red:**

Cut two of Pattern 6

**White:**

Cut two of Pattern 2
Cut two of Pattern 4
Cut one of Pattern 7

*148*

Cut two of Pattern 8
Cut one of Pattern 9
Cut two of Pattern 11
Cut two of Pattern 12

STEP 1

First sew a 2 on each side of 1, checking diagram.

Then put a row of machine stitching on the sewing line of both 2-1-2 and 3 separately. Sew only the curves of each piece.

Set 3 into 2-1-2 by matching notches and pinning. Be sure the notches are clipped all the way to the sewing line. Baste.

Sew 3 to 2-1-2 all around the curve, smoothing out the fabric and adjusting as you go. Press seam away from 3.

If you find you need to, refer to the preceding instructions for *Set-in Curves*.

STEP 2

Check diagram carefully through each of the following steps:

Sew a 4 to each side of 5, end to end.

Sew the two red 6 pieces between the three black 6 pieces lengthwise so the colors alternate, with black at the outer sides.

Sew 7 to the right side of the row of 6s.

Sew a white 8 to either side of the black 8 end to end.

Sew 9 to 10 side by side.

Sew a 12 to each side of 13, end to end.

Press everything. If the fabric is somewhat sheer, press seams away from the white so that the colors won't show through.

STEP 3

Sew 4-5 along the bottom of 1-2-3.

Sew all the 8 pieces to the left side of the row of 6s.

Sew an 11 to the top and bottom of 9-10.

Press everything.

STEP 4

Sew 9-10-11 to the left of 8.

Sew this entire section to the bottom of section 1-2-3-4-5.

Sew 12-13 to the bottom of the entire piece.

Press the hydrant on the wrong side first, then on the right side.

*149*

**FIRE HYDRANT**

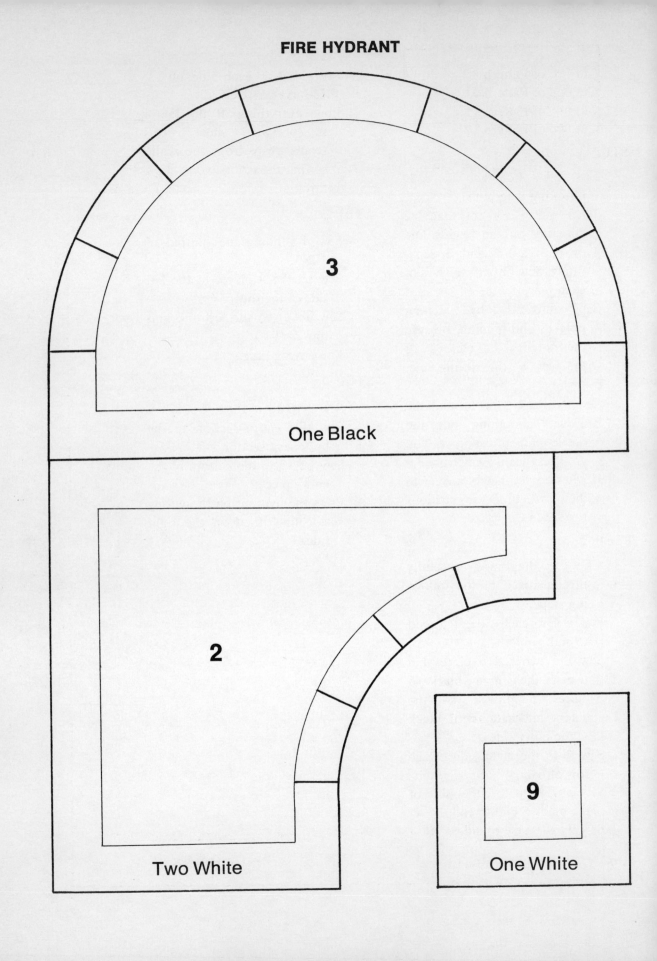

3

One Black

2

Two White

9

One White

**FIRE HYDRANT**

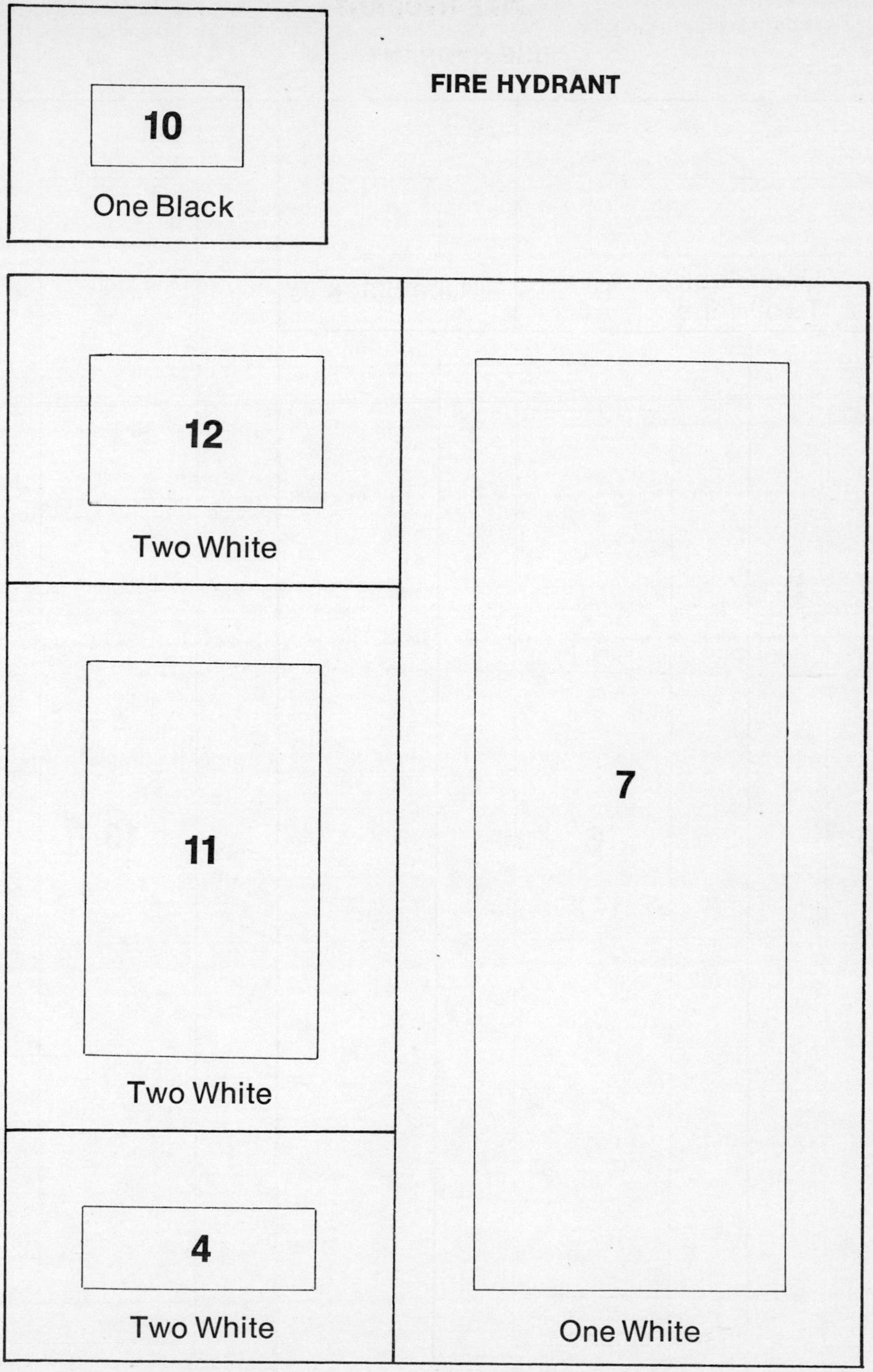

| 10 |
|---|
| One Black |

| 12 |
|---|
| Two White |

| 11 |
|---|
| Two White |

| 4 |
|---|
| Two White |

| 7 |
|---|
| One White |

# FIRE HYDRANT

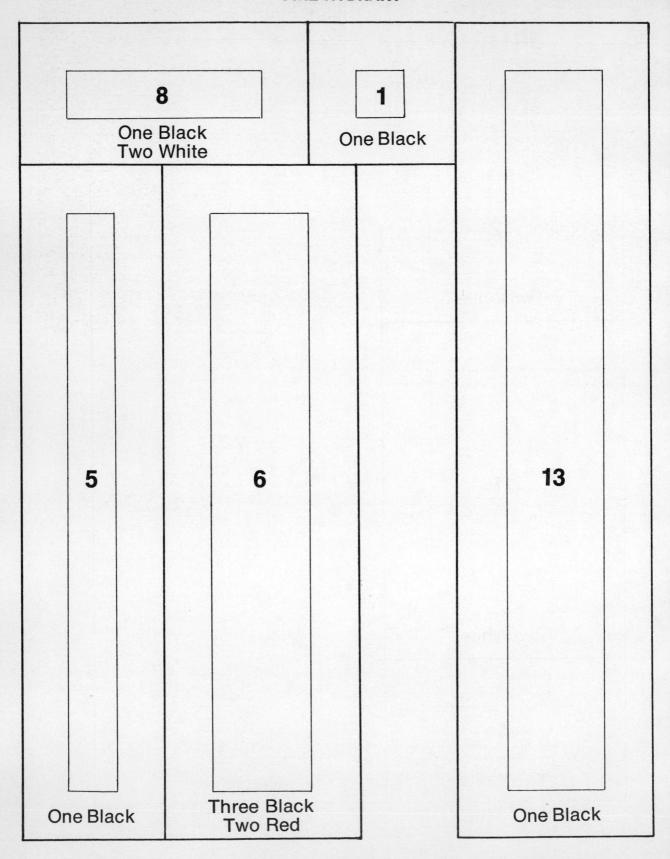

**8**

One Black
Two White

**1**

One Black

**5**

One Black

**6**

Three Black
Two Red

**13**

One Black

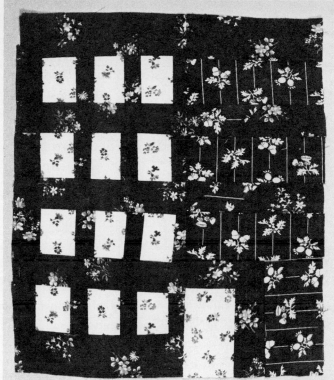

**TENEMENT**

| 11 | | | | | | | 1 | |
|---|---|---|---|---|---|---|---|---|
| 9 | 10 | 9 | 10 | 9 | 10 | 9 | 2 | |
| 11 | | | | | | 3 | 4 | 5 |
| 9 | 10 | 9 | 10 | 9 | 10 | 9 | 2 | |
| 11 | | | | | | 3 | 4 | 5 |
| 9 | 10 | 9 | 10 | 9 | 10 | 9 | 2 | |
| 11 | | | | | | | 7 | |
| 9 | 10 | 9 | 10 | 9 | 10 | 9 | 8 | |
| 11 | | | | | | 6 | 7 | |

# TENEMENT

Suggested Colors: Blue, Blue and White Stripe, White

**Blue:**

Cut one of Pattern 1
* Cut two of Pattern 3
* Cut two of Pattern 5
Cut two of Pattern 7
Cut eight of Pattern 9
Cut five of Pattern 11

**\*\* Blue and White Stripe:**

Cut three of Pattern 2
Cut two of Pattern 4
Cut one of Pattern 8

**White:**

Cut one of Pattern 6
Cut six of Pattern 10

\* The 3 and 5 pieces may be cut from two layers of fabric placed one on top of the other and cut as one, but both pieces must be *right side up*.

\*\* When placing pattern pieces 2, 4, and 8 on the striped fabric be sure the stripe in the pattern is the same direction as the stripe in the fabric.

## STEP 1

Sew 1 to one of the 2 pieces, lengthwise.
Sew 4 between 3 and 5, matching notches. Repeat.
Sew 6 to a 7 along the longest side.
Sew the other 7 along the top of 6-7 (door).
Press everything.

## STEP 2

Sew 3-4-5 between two 2 pieces. Repeat, checking diagram as you go.
Sew 8 down the right side of 6-7-7.
Sew 6-7-8 to the bottom of the 2-3-4-5 section.
Press. This completes the fire escape section.

## STEP 3

Sew three 10 pieces between four 9 pieces lengthwise. Repeat.
Press all the seams in one direction.
Fold these two 9-10 sections neatly in half and press this fold into a crease. Cut both sections in half along the crease. You now have your rows of windows.

## STEP 4

Sew each row of windows lengthwise between the five pieces of 11.
Press.
Sew the window section to the fire escape section and the tenement is finished. Give a final press on the wrong and right sides.

Optional: Embroider an address on the door and window boxes with flowers in the windows.

**TENEMENT**

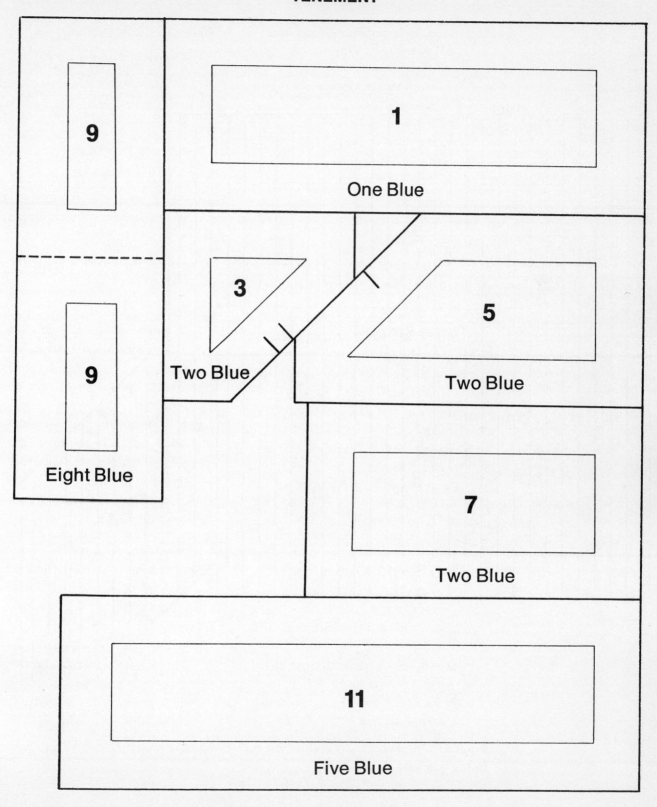

9

1

One Blue

3

5

Two Blue

Two Blue

9

7

Eight Blue

Two Blue

11

Five Blue

# TENEMENT

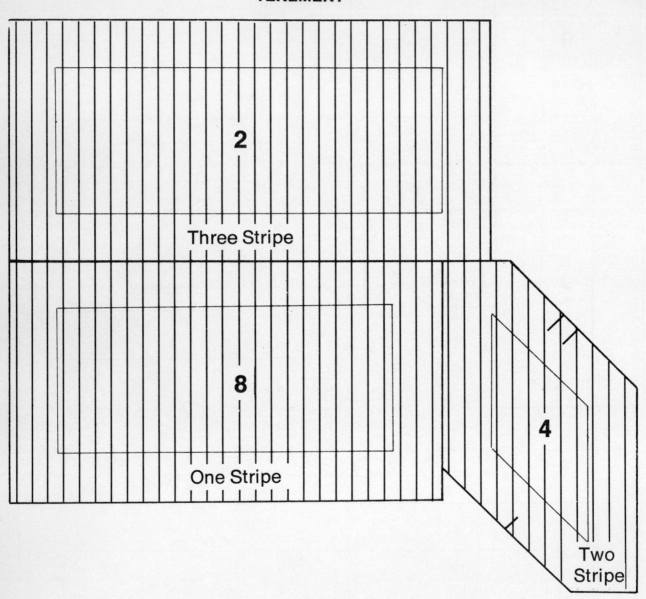

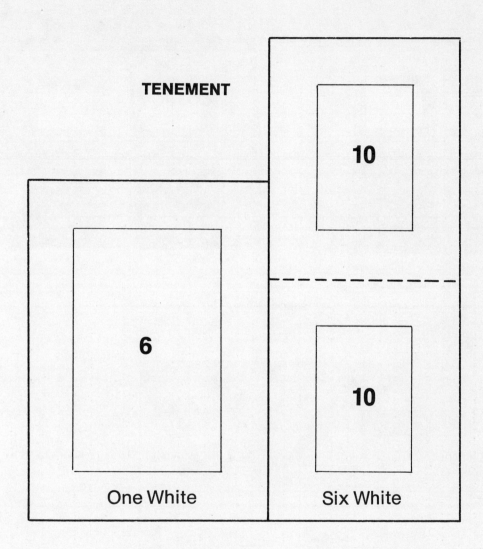

**TENEMENT**

6

10

10

One White

Six White

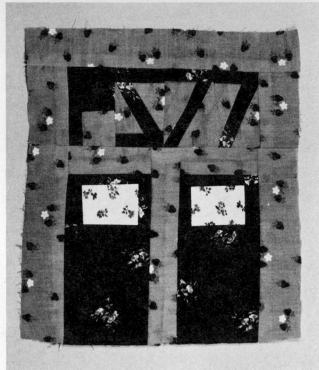

## SCHOOL

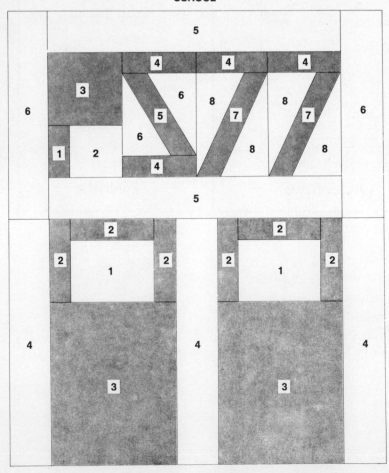

# SCHOOL PS 77

This is a pattern in two parts. The sign is optional. If you want to leave it out, replace with a piece of red measuring 6 by 10 inches. This will also eliminate 5 and 6 of the school pattern. Then embroider a sign or design your own patchwork sign, making the patterns using the patternmaking instructions in Chapter 3.

**Sign**

Suggested Colors: Red, Blue

**Red:**

Cut one of Pattern 2
* Cut two of Pattern 6
* Cut four of Pattern 8

**Blue:**

Cut one of Pattern 1
Cut one of Pattern 3
Cut four of Pattern 4
Cut one of Pattern 5
Cut two of Pattern 7

* 6 and 8 must be cut from two layers of fabric, both facing right side up.

P: Sew 2 to 1 lengthwise.
Sew 3 on top of 1 and 2 so that 2 is on the right side.

S: Sew a 6 on each side of 5, matching notches. Press.
Sew a 4 on the top and bottom of 5-6.

7: Sew an 8 on each side of 7, matching notches. Press.
Sew a 4 on top of 7-8.
Repeat for the second 7.

Press everything and sew the numbers and letters together. Press again.

# SIGN PS 77

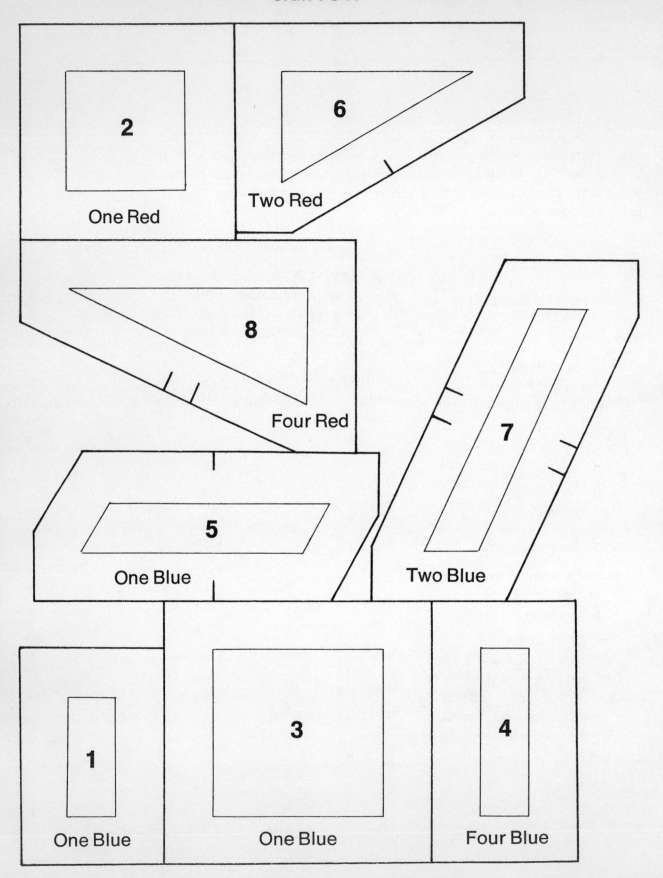

**2** One Red

**6** Two Red

**8** Four Red

**7** Two Blue

**5** One Blue

**1** One Blue

**3** One Blue

**4** Four Blue

**School**

Suggested Colors: Red, White, Blue

**Red:**

>   Cut three of Pattern 4
>   Cut two of Pattern 5
>   Cut two of Pattern 6

**White:**

>   Cut two of Pattern 1

**Blue:**

>   Cut six of Pattern 2
>   Cut two of Pattern 3

STEP 1

>   Sew 2s on top and sides of each
>     1 as shown in diagram.
>   Press.

STEP 2

>   Sew a 3 on the bottom of each
>     1-2.
>   Sew both groups of 1-2-3 be-
>     tween the three pieces of 4.
>   Sew the 5s on the top and bot-
>     tom of the PS 77 sign.
>   Press.

STEP 3

>   Sew a 6 on each side of the PS
>     77 sign.
>   Sew the sign to the school.

**SCHOOL**

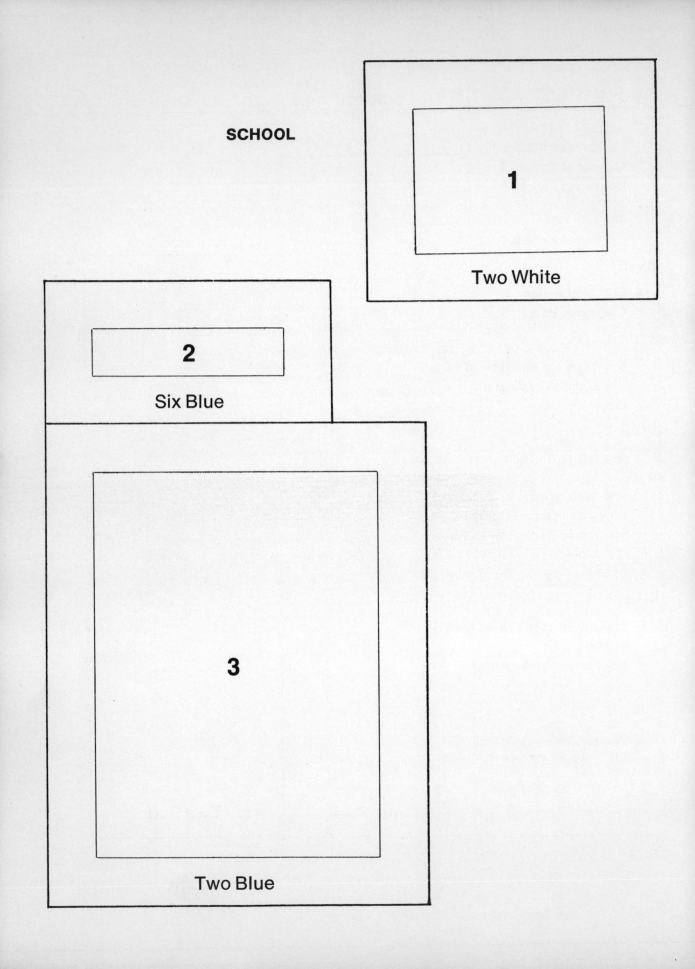

**1**

Two White

**2**

Six Blue

**3**

Two Blue

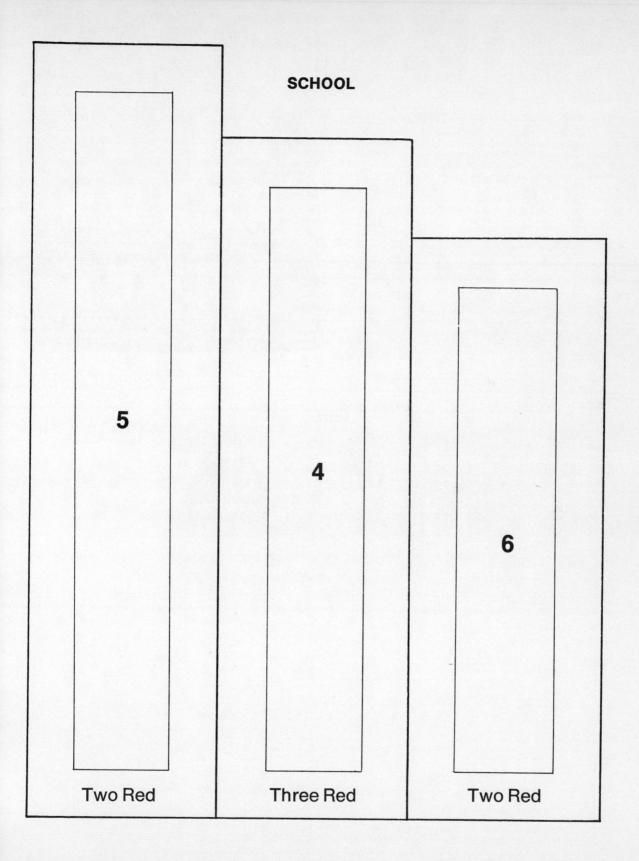

SCHOOL

5

4

6

Two Red

Three Red

Two Red

## HOTEL

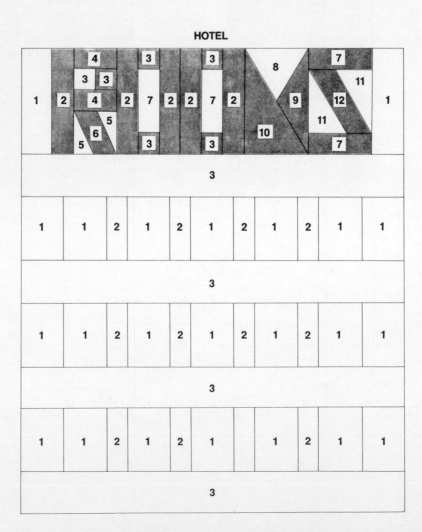

# HOTEL

This pattern is in two parts: the sign and the building are numbered separately. If you choose to leave out the sign replace it with a piece of green 3½ by 10 inches. This can be embroidered or left plain. If you wish to replace it with a patchwork pattern of your own, follow the patternmaking directions described in Chapter 3.

## Sign

I have made each letter a different color, but all can be the same color, as in the instructions given. If you want each letter different, be sure to choose colors which will be in contrast to the background. I have drawn Pattern 3 and 7, which are cut from both colors, twice.

Suggested Colors: Green, Red

### Green:

Cut two of Pattern 1
Cut one of Pattern 3
* Cut two of Pattern 5
Cut two of Pattern 7
Cut one of Pattern 8
* Cut two of Pattern 11

### Red:

Cut five of Pattern 2
Cut five of Pattern 3
Cut two of Pattern 4
Cut one of Pattern 6
Cut two of Pattern 7
Cut one of Pattern 9
Cut one of Pattern 10
Cut one of Pattern 12

* Both 5 and 11 are cut on two layers of fabric both right side up.

R: Sew a 1 to a 2.
Sew a green 3 to a red 3. Press.
Sew 4s on the top and bottom of the two Pattern 3 pieces.
Sew a 5 on either side of 6, matching notches.
Press the last two pieces.
Sew 5-6 to the bottom of 3-4.
Sew 1-2 to the right of 3-4-5-6.

O: For both Os sew a 3 on each end of 7, end to end. Press.
Sew the 3-7 pieces between two red 2 pieces.

M: Sew 8 to 9, matching notches. Press.
Sew 10 to 8-9, matching notches.

S: Sew an 11 on each side of 12, matching notches. Press.
Sew red 7s on the top and bottom of 11-12.

Press all the letters and sew together. Press again.

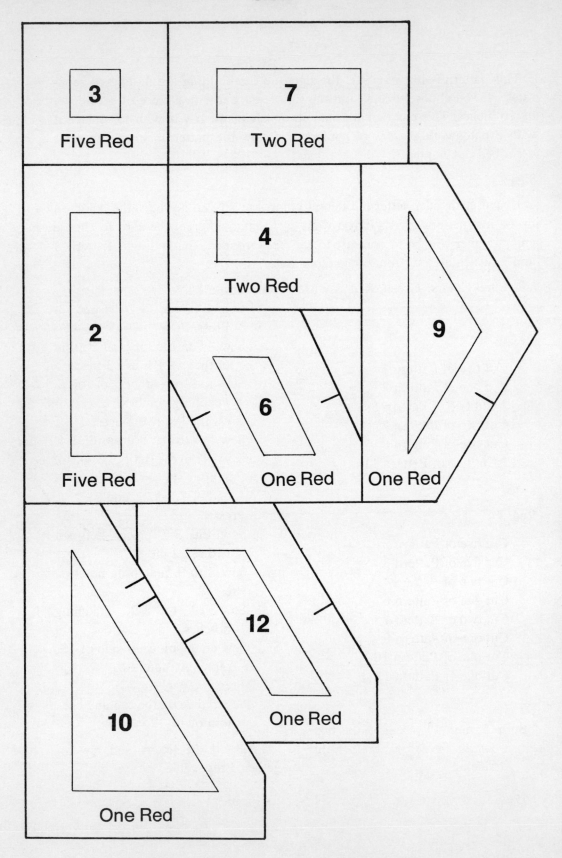

**SIGN**

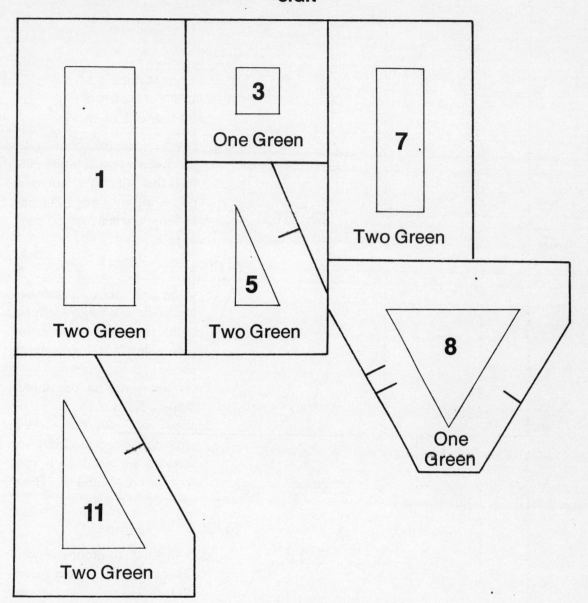

### Hotel

Suggested Colors: White, Green

**White:**

Cut five of Pattern 1

**Green:**

Cut two of Pattern 1
Cut four of Pattern 2
* Cut four of Pattern 3

* 3 is drawn on the fold of the fabric. Keep in mind while cutting that all four Pattern 3 pieces will measure 10 inches in length when cut on fold of fabric.

### STEP 1

Sew the four green 2 pieces between the five white 1 pieces.
Sew the two green 1 pieces on both sides of 1-2 completed above.
Press the seams in one direction.
Measure and cut this section into three equal 2½-inch sections as marked on pattern pieces 1 and 2. These are the windows.

### STEP 2

Sew these three groups of windows between the four pieces of 3.
Press.

### STEP 3

Sew the hotel to the ROOMS sign.
Press on both sides.

**HOTEL**

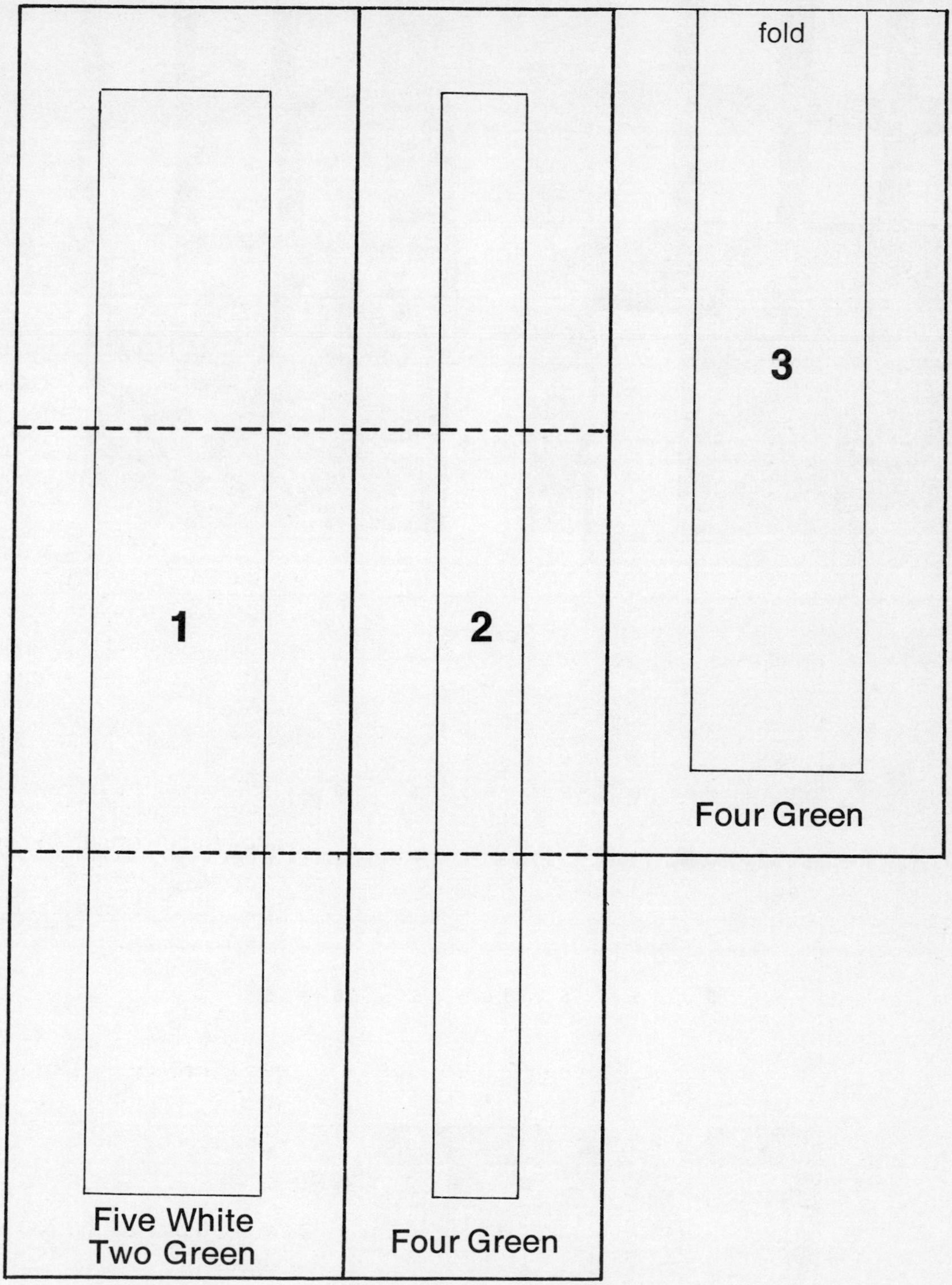

**1**

**2**

**3**

fold

Four Green

Five White
Two Green

Four Green

**CAFE**

| 7 | | | | | | |
|---|---|---|---|---|---|---|
| 5 | 6 | 5 | 6 | 5 | 6 | 5 |

8 | 7 | 8

| 5 | 6 | 5 | 6 | 5 | 6 | 5 |
|---|---|---|---|---|---|---|

7

# CAFE

The sign and the building are numbered as two separate patterns. The sign is optional; if you choose to leave it out replace with a brown block measuring 3¼ by 7½ inches. Or make your own patchwork pattern.

## Cafe Sign

Suggested Colors: Red, Brown

**Red:**

Cut three of Pattern 1
Cut seven of Pattern 3
Cut one of Pattern 4

**Brown:**

Cut one of Pattern 1
Cut one of Pattern 2
Cut three of Pattern 3
* Cut two of Pattern 5
Cut one of Pattern 6

* 5 must be cut from two layers of fabric, both right side up.

C: Sew a 3 to each end of 2.
Sew a red 1 down the left side of 2-3.
A: Sew a 5 on either side of 4, matching notches.
F: Sew a red 3 on either side of a brown 3.
Sew 6 on the bottom of the row of 3s finished above.
Sew a red 1 down the left side of 3-6.

E: Sew the remaining 3 pieces together alternating red and brown so that there are two brown 3s between three red 3s.
Sew a red 1 down the left side of this row of 3s.
Sew a brown 1 down the right side.

Press each letter and sew together to spell CAFE. Press again on both sides.

# CAFE SIGN

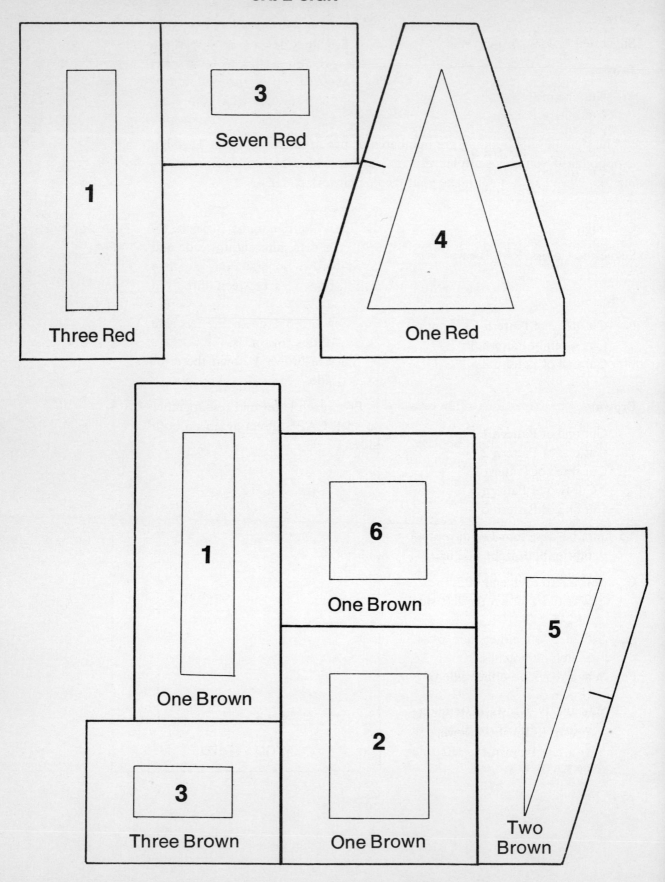

**1** Three Red

**3** Seven Red

**4** One Red

**1** One Brown

**6** One Brown

**3** Three Brown

**2** One Brown

**5** Two Brown

## Cafe

Suggested Colors: Brown, White

**Brown:**

Cut one of Pattern 2
Cut one of Pattern 3
Cut one of Pattern 4
Cut three of Pattern 6
Cut three of Pattern 7
Cut two of Pattern 8

**White:**

Cut one of Pattern 1
Cut four of Pattern 5

### STEP 1

Sew 2 to the top of 1.
Sew 3 down the right side of 1-2.
Sew 4 to the bottom of the cafe sign.
Sew the three 6 pieces between the four 5 pieces lengthwise.
Press everything. Fold the 5-6 piece in half neatly and press the fold into a crease. Cut along this crease (the dotted line indicated in the pattern pieces 5 and 6). You now have two rows of windows.

### STEP 2

Sew the cafe sign to the door (1-2-3).
Sew the two rows of windows between the three pieces of 7.
Press everything.

### STEP 3

Sew an 8 down each side of the window section (5-6-7).
Sew the top of the building to the bottom with the cafe sign.
Press on both sides.

**CAFE**

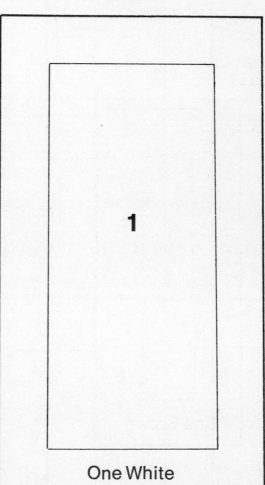

One White

173

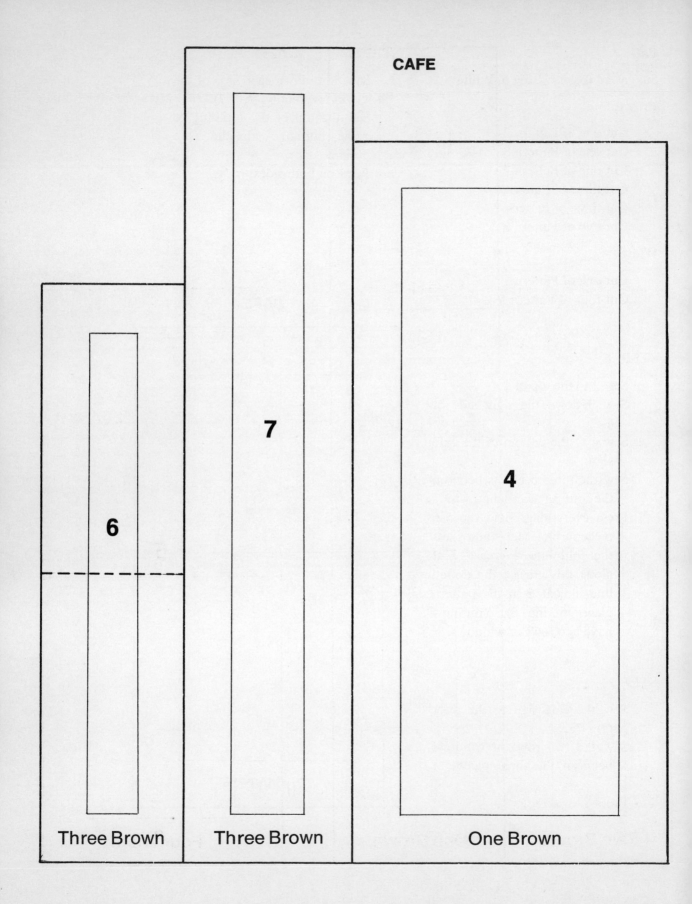

CAFE

6

7

4

Three Brown

Three Brown

One Brown

**CAFE**

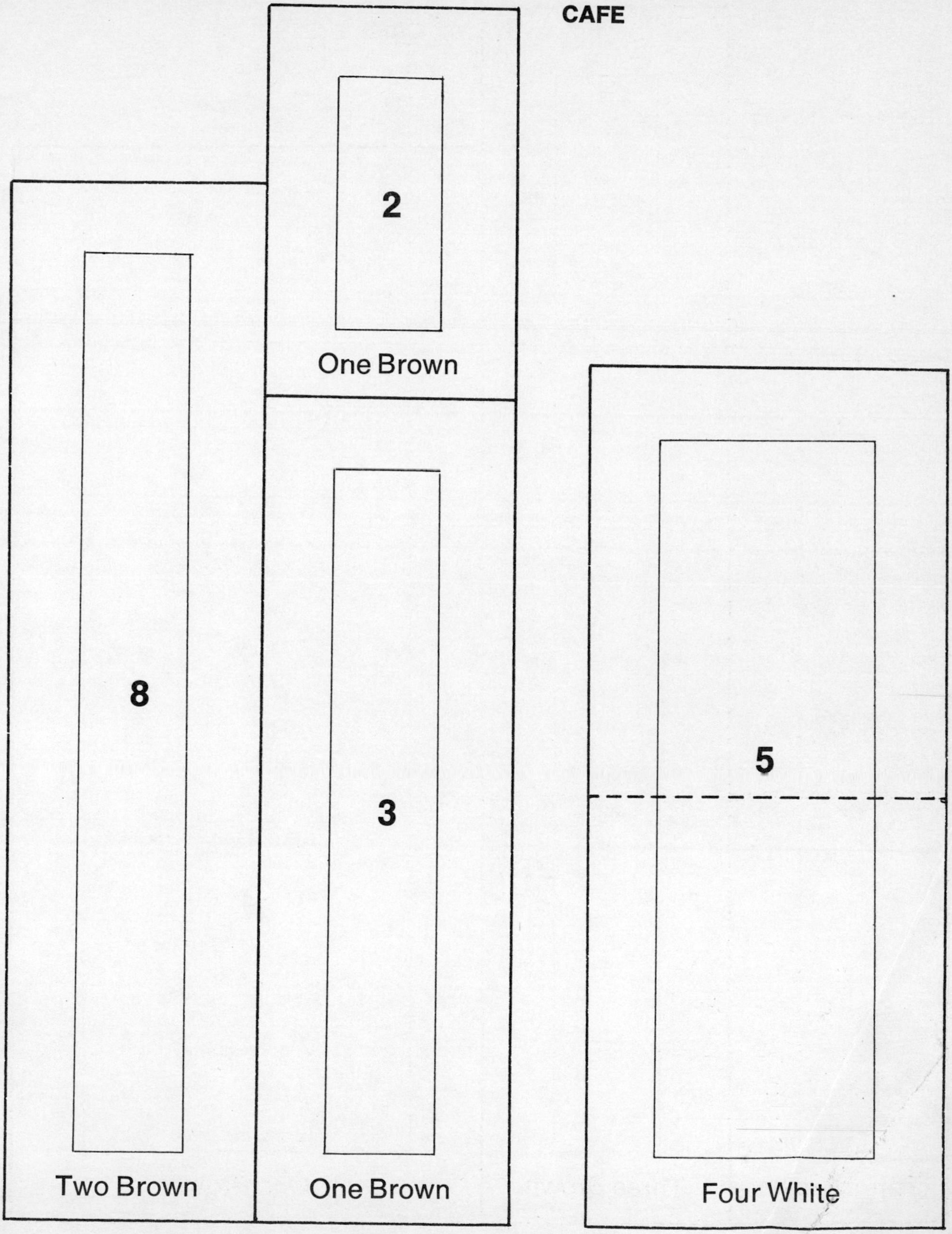

**2**

One Brown

**8**

**3**

**5**

Two Brown

One Brown

Four White